QUALITY CONTROL

FOR OPERATORS & FOREMEN

QUALITY CONTROL

FOR OPERATORS & FOREMEN

K.S. KRISHNAMOORTHI

ASQC QUALITY PRESS

QUALITY CONTROL FOR OPERATORS & FOREMEN

K.S. KRISHNAMOORTHI

Acquisitions Editor: Jeanine L. Lau
Production Editor: Tammy Griffin
Cover design by Artistic License, Inc. Set in Triumvirate by DanTon Typographers.
Printed and bound by BookCrafters.

109876543

ISBN 0-87389-048-5

Printed in the United States of America

  Printed on Recycled Paper

ASQC
Quality Press
611 East Wisconsin Avenue
Milwaukee, Wisconsin 53202

To the memory of my parents:
Subramania Iyer
Nagalakshmi

CONTENTS

PREFACE

This book is the result of experience gained from teaching several quality control classes for line personnel, and is expected to meet the needs of those quality control engineers and managers who want to train their line people themselves.

There have been several books on quality control published in the last two years, but most seem to be directed at the white-collar audience or the college student. This book specifically addresses the questions and concerns of line people.

Effective on-line quality control depends on the successful education of the line personnel and convincing them about the usefulness and usability of the control procedures. The statement attributed to Dr. H. F. Dodge that "statistical quality control is 10 percent statistics and 90 percent engineering," can be rephrased as "statistical quality control is 10 percent statistics, 10 percent engineering, and 80 percent 'mechanics,'" meaning that operators, mechanics, and foremen contribute 80 percent toward a good statistical quality control program. It is because of this they need special attention.

I have kept the writing practical and readable. Wherever possible I have tried to give insight into the methods to explain why a method works the way it does. Most people want such insight and appreciate it. I have also tried to answer some of the usual questions that arise in the classroom where this book may be used.

The entire book can be covered in about 25 contact hours if all participants have had high school mathematics. The time needed may vary if the educational preparation of the participants is different. The first nine chapters which relate to statistical process control can be covered in 20 hours.

The best class length is an hour and a half, with the last 30 to 40 minutes being devoted to in-class workshops. The instructor should work individually with participants during the workshops. This is where the learning takes place and where many questions are answered. If the instructor can build on examples from the places of work of the participants, these workshops are the starting points for implementation of statistical process control in the workplace. Because of the individual attention needed during the workshops, the optimal class size is about 20 students.

I would appreciate receiving any comments, corrections, or improvements that may make future editions of this book more valuable.

K.S.K.
Peoria, Illinois
July 1988

CHAPTER ONE: INTRODUCTION

This book is devoted primarily to the process control methods used in process improvements. Chapters One through Nine are devoted to this topic, while Chapter Ten covers the basics of sampling plans.

OVERVIEW

Chapter One: Introduction

- What is quality?
- What is quality control?
- Why do we need statistics?

This chapter lays the foundation and establishes the language for the remaining chapters.

Chapter Two: Mathematics Review

- Decimal arithmetic
- Average, range
- Formula simplification

Chapter Two contains the math that will be needed for quality control work. A little effort here saves a lot of effort later.

Chapter Three: Control Charts

- Concept of control charts
- Benefits from control charts

A general discussion of the basics of control charts and what they can do is discussed in this chapter. This chapter should also answer the question, "Why should we use control charts?"

Chapter Four: X-Bar and R-Charts

- Computation of limits
- Plotting data
- Interpretation of charts

This is the most important chapter. A detailed discussion of X-bar and R-charts is given since these are the most used and most useful tools.

Chapter Five: Attribute Control Charts

- p-chart
- c-chart

This is a continuation of the previous chapter. Two attribute charts are described. These tools may be useful for some readers.

Chapter Six: Special Control Charts

- Moving average charts
- Moving range charts

These charts are simple variations of X-bar and R-charts. They are easy to learn and easy to use. They are useful for chemical processes.

Chapter Seven: Frequency Distributions

- Method of drawing histograms
- Interpretation of histograms

A histogram provides a picture of the capability of a process. Modern computer software for quality control puts out pictures of distributions. We should be able to interpret them.

Chapter Eight: Numerical Methods to Describe Populations

- Measures for central tendency
- Measures for variability

These are measures statisticians have created to describe what is in a process. These are needed to measure process capability.

Chapter Nine: Normal Distribution and Process Capability

- Normal distribution
- Cp and Cpk indices

This topic is somewhat advanced, but these are becoming common knowledge. Capability indices are used to assess how good a process is.

Chapter Ten: Sampling Plans

- Single sampling plans for attributes
- MIL-STD-105D

The fundamentals of single sampling plans are explained along with instructions on how to select plans from MIL-STD-105D.

WHAT IS QUALITY?

A product is said to have *quality* when it satisfies the customer's intended use. The quality of a product is determined by the specifications of several *quality characteristics* of the product. The designer designs a quality product by choosing specifications which he or she believes will satisfy the customer's needs. The production people try to make the product to meet the chosen specifications.

Two products could have a difference in their quality because of the difference in the quality designed for them.

A Cadillac and a Chevette have differences in quality because there are differences in their designed quality, i.e. differences in their specifications. Two products with the same *design quality* (same specifications) could have a difference in quality because they conformed to the specifications in different degrees when they were manufactured. A well-made Chevette has better quality than a poorly made Chevette because of the difference in their conformance to specifications.

In this book we will concentrate primarily on this latter quality, referred to as *quality of conformance* or manufacturing quality. In other words, making quality products means making products to specifications.

QUALITY CONTROL IS TEAMWORK

The quality of a product depends on many factors and activities of many agencies in a company:

1. Incoming Material
   - Buying quality material
   - Performing incoming inspection
   - Storing material properly

2. Production Process
   - Tools and machinery that are capable of producing quality products
   - Workers who are trained properly
   - Properly maintained instruments that are capable of measuring desired accuracy
   - In-process inspection and control procedures for controlling the process

3. Final Inspection and Shipping
   - Verification that the product meets specifications
   - Proper packaging and shipping

All of these activities fall into the quality control function in a plant. Thus, quality control involves many functions at many places. It is the *teamwork* performed by many people.

QUALITY CONTROL IS PREVENTION OF DEFECTIVES

We should note that final inspection is just one function of total quality control activities. Final inspection alone cannot produce a quality product. *You cannot inspect quality into a product.*

A quality control system should aim at making the product *right the first time*. Scrap and rework cost money. When these costs are added to the price of a good product, it loses its competitive position in the market. Loss of sales leads to loss of jobs. This is what has been plaguing many American industries that have lost business to foreign competition (Figure 1.1).

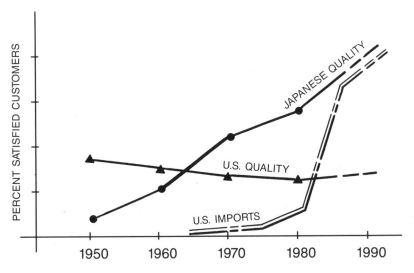

FIGURE 1.1 JAPANESE QUALITY ON THE INCREASE — U.S. QUALITY ON THE DECLINE

When there is no scrap or rework, there is more good product to sell. Materials, machine time, and manpower are not wasted on rework. Productivity goes up when quality improves (Figure 1.2).

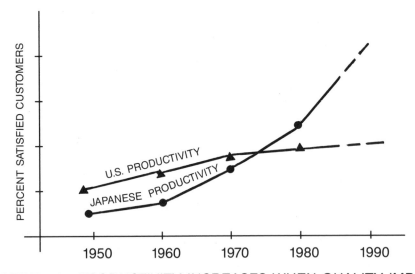

FIGURE 1.2 PRODUCTIVITY INCREASES WHEN QUALITY IMPROVES

When overhead is spread over a greater number of products, there will be less cost per unit, more profit, a better market share, more business, and lasting jobs. Figure 1.3 illustrates this.

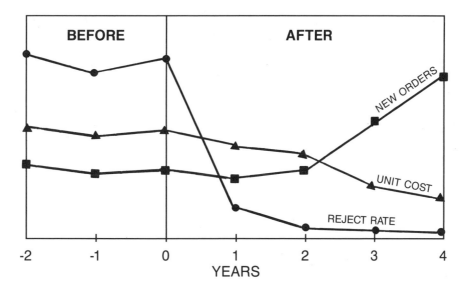

FIGURE 1.3 TYPICAL RESULTS OF A QUALITY IMPROVEMENT PROGRAM

A good quality control plan should aim for *prevention of defectives*. The simple process control methods discussed in this book will help us to see when a process is producing good product and when it is not. When a process is not producing quality, it can be corrected. Many companies have used these methods and have benefited from them. There is a quality revolution taking place in American industry today through the use of simple statistical methods that are powerful tools for controlling processes.

WHY STATISTICS?

Statistics is the science that helps in the evaluation of populations by looking at samples. A *population* is made up of all the items that are of interest in a given situation. Examples of this include the following:

- Population of all bags filled in line 2 during the first shift.
- Population of all tubing received from a given supplier in a day.
- Population of all labels cut on press 6 in a week.

A *sample* is a part of the population taken in such a way that it is representative of the population. A sample may be made up of just one item, or several items, or one pound of powder, or half a pint of liquid, etc.

The term *subgroup* is often used in place of sample when we want to make it clear that the sample consists of more than one item. The terms *sample* and *subgroup* are used synonomously.

Samples should be taken *randomly* so that the sample is representative of the population. Randomness can be interpreted as having no planned pattern or order in picking the items of the sample. For example, if a random sample of five eggs from a carton of 100 eggs is needed, all five eggs shouldn't be picked from the top or bottom row, or from one corner. A sample taken randomly is called a *random sample*.

VARIABILITY

Every population, natural or man-made, has *variability*. This is the same as saying that no two items in a population are alike. No two persons have the same weight; no two cans of beer have the same amount of beer in them, no two batches of chemical produced in the same reactor have the same amount of impurity. Even items that seem identical will be seen as different if you look closely enough or use a more accurate measuring instrument.

The tolerances given in the specifications are meant to recognize this variability. It is this variability that makes evaluation of the quality of a population of products difficult. If a population has no variability, inspection of one item from the population will determine whether the lot is good or bad. If there *is* variability, it is not easy to measure the quality of a lot by looking at the quality of a sample (Figure 1.4). This is where statistics is needed; it gives us methods to describe this variability and help in relating the quality of a sample to the quality of a lot.

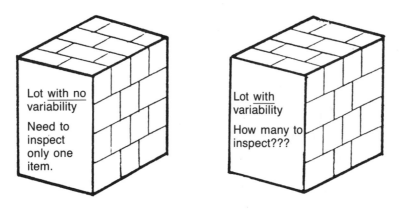

FIGURE 1.4 VARIABILITY IN POPULATIONS CAUSES PROBLEMS IN JUDGING QUALITY

All the populations dealt with in industry have variability. In many situations we must use samples to evaluate the population of products. Thus, statistical tools become a necessary component of quality control programs.

TWO STATISTICAL METHODS

Statistical quality control methods can be divided into two groups as shown in Table 1.1. Since control charts are useful as tools to *prevent* poor quality, they are needed in a quality control program where prevention of defectives is the hallmark. These are also referred to as statistical process control (SPC) methods.

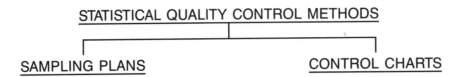

STATISTICAL QUALITY CONTROL METHODS

SAMPLING PLANS

- Used by customer after production
- Results in accept/reject decision of products

CONTROL CHARTS

- Used by producer during production
- Results in process improvement to prevent defectives

TABLE 1.1 TWO STATISTICAL METHODS

TWO TYPES OF DATA

There are two types of data arising from inspection:

1. Attribute Data
2. Variable or Measurement Data

Attribute data are obtained when products are classified into two or three categories, such as good/bad, tight/loose, minor/major/serious, underweight/overweight, etc.

Example

This is what attribute data look like:

- Three percent defectives
- Two out of 10 have bad color

Variable (or measurement) data are obtained when a measurement such as weight, length, amount of impurity, or strength is made on the product.

Example

This is what variable data look like:

- 2.5 lbs
- 320 psi
- 22 ppm
- 2.16 in

We need to know what type of data we have in a given situation in order to select an appropriate statistical quality control method, since the particular method to be used depends on the type of data.

There are sampling plans for attribute inspection and there are sampling plans for variable inspection. There are control charts for attribute inspection and there are control charts for variable inspection. These statistical tools will be discussed in subsequent chapters.

REVIEW

What is quality?
What is quality control?
Why do we need statistics?
What is a population?
What is a sample?
What is a random sample?
Variability in populations
Two methods of statistical quality control:

- Control charts
- Sampling plans

Two types of data:

- Attribute data
- Variable data

CHAPTER TWO: MATHEMATICS REVIEW

This chapter will review some basic mathematical operations needed in the use of statistical quality control methods.

PROPORTIONS

Proportion of rejects in a population or sample can be expressed as a:

- Common fraction (e.g., $\frac{3}{16}$)

- Decimal fraction (e.g., 0.1875)

- Percentage (e.g., 18.75 percent)

Example

An inspector opens a box containing six bottles and finds that two of them have bad labels. What proportion of the bottles in the box have bad labels?

$$\text{Answer: } \frac{2}{6} = 0.333 = 33.3\%$$

We will use decimal fractions for proportions in most of our work.

ADDITION AND SUBTRACTION OF DECIMAL FRACTIONS

Addition and subtraction are easily figured using modern calculators. Everyone who works with SPC methods should be comfortable in using calculators.

Example

Add:	1.5	2.5
	0.032	−0.8
	4.01	1.9
	12.0	−3.2
	17.542	0.4

DECIMAL MULTIPLICATION

Example

$$3.25 \times 0.577 = 1.87525$$
$$2.114 \times 1.4 = 2.9596$$

With decimal multiplication, as with division, the results may need to be rounded off to a desired number of significant places. Rounding off is done by looking at the digit next to the last significant place desired. If that number is five or greater, add one to the last significant place. If it is four or less, truncate at the last significant place.

Example

$$3.25 \times 0.577 = 1.875 \text{ (rounded to the thousandth)}$$

DECIMAL DIVISION

Example

$$\frac{1.45}{2.326} = 0.6234 \text{ (rounded to the ten thousandth)}$$

$$\frac{1.45}{2.326} = 0.623 \text{ (rounded to the thousandth)}$$

COMPUTING THE AVERAGE

Suppose the following numbers are diameters (in inches) of five shafts turned in an automatic lathe:

1.245, 1.247, 1.244, 1.246, 1.243

Then, the average diameter:

$$= \frac{(\text{sum of the 5 measurements})}{5}$$

$$= \frac{(1.245 + 1.247 + 1.244 + 1.246 + 1.243)}{5}$$

$$= 1.245$$

General formula for average:

$$\overline{X} = \frac{\Sigma X}{n}$$

Where:
$\overline{X}$ – (X-bar) is the notation used for the average
X represents the typical value in the data
ΣX is the sum of the observations in data
n = number of observations in data (also called the *sample size*)

A Note About Summation Notation

Σ is the Greek letter (capital sigma) that is the equivalent of S for sum. This notation makes it easy while writing formulas for averages and other quantities that we will be computing.

COMPUTING THE RANGE

The range of a set of data, denoted by R, is the difference between the largest and the smallest observation.

Example

Find the range of the data.

$$\begin{array}{ccccc} & H & & & L \\ 1.245 & 1.247 & 1.244 & 1.246 & 1.243 \end{array}$$

$$R = (1.247 - 1.243) = 0.004$$

(Note that it is a good idea to mark the high and low values to avoid error.)

SQUARE AND SQUARE ROOT OF NUMBERS

The square of a number is the result of multiplying the number by itself. The symbol for the square is the exponent 2 written as a superscript to the number.

Example

$$2^2 \text{ (2 square)} = 2 \times 2 = 4$$
$$1.5^2 \text{ (1.5 square)} = 1.5 \times 1.5 = 2.25$$

The square root of a number is that number whose square is the original number. The symbol for square root is the radical sign $\sqrt{}$.

Example

$$\sqrt{9} = 3 \text{ (because } 3^2 = 9)$$
$$\sqrt{36} = 6$$
$$\sqrt{44} = 6.6332$$
$$\sqrt{676} = 26$$

There are mathematical methods that can be used to obtain the square root of any given number. However, we will use the calculator to find the square root of numbers.

FORMULA SIMPLIFICATION

We may have to use several formulas in the use of statistical methods, and we must know how to derive their values. The following rules are used and their use is shown in the examples:

Rule 1

If there are additions, subtractions, multiplications, and divisions in a formula, the multiplications and divisions should be done first and then the additions and subtractions.

Rule 2

If there are quantities inside parentheses, they must be simplified first.

Rule 3

If there are several sets of parentheses, the quantity within the inner-most set must be simplified first, then we should work outward.

Example A

Find the value of U.

$$U = X + A \times R, \text{ where } X = 20, A = 0.57, R = 4$$
$$U = 20 + 0.57 \times 4$$
$$= 20 + 2.28$$
$$= 22.28$$

When writing formulas the multiplication sign is sometimes not written explicitly. The following examples use the implied multiplication sign.

Example B

Find the value of U.

$$U = X + AR, \text{ where } X = 20, A = 0.57, R = 4$$
$$U = 20 + 0.57 \times 4 = 22.28$$

Example C

Find the value of V.

$$V = X + 3\sqrt{Y}, \text{ where } X = 20, Y = 16$$
$$V = 20 + 3\sqrt{16} = 20 + 3 \times 4 = 32$$

Example D

Find the value of W.

$$W = 2(A + B) + 3(B - A), \text{ where } A = 2, B = 6$$
$$W = 2 \times 8 + 3 \times 4 = 28$$

Example E

Find the value of W.

$$W = 3\sqrt{\frac{p(1 - p)}{n}}, \text{ where } p = .3, n = 64$$
$$= 3\sqrt{\frac{.3(1 - .3)}{64}}$$
$$= 3\sqrt{\frac{.3(.7)}{64}}$$
$$= 3\sqrt{.00328125}$$
$$= 3 \times .0572821961$$
$$= 0.1718465886$$

Example F

In calculating control limits for what is called the p-chart, we use the following formulas:

$$UCL = \bar{p} + 3\sqrt{\frac{\bar{p}(1 - \bar{p})}{n}}$$

$$LCL = \bar{p} - 3\sqrt{\frac{\bar{p}(1 - \bar{p})}{n}}$$

11

Calculate the upper control limit (UCL) and lower control limit (LCL) for a value of:

$$\bar{p} = 0.45 \text{ and } n = 50$$

$$UCL = 0.45 + 3\sqrt{\frac{(0.45)(0.55)}{50}} = 0.6611$$

$$LCL = 0.45 - 3\sqrt{\frac{(0.45)(0.55)}{50}} = 0.2389$$

This is probably the most difficult formula that will be encountered in SPC.

CODING

Coding of data is done to obtain round numbers to work with when the numbers in the data are too small or too large. Coding is done by subtracting a constant quantity from all the observations in data, or multiplying all observations by a constant, or both.

Example A

Original data (X)	Coded data (X − 250)
248	−2
252	+2
256	+6 H
246	−4 L
250	0

Example B

Original data (X)	Coded data (X × 1000)
.004	4
.008	8
.006	6
.002	2 L
.009	9 H

Example C

Original data (X)	Coded data (X − 1.24) × 1000
1.245	5
1.247	7 H
1.244	4
1.246	6
1.243	3 L

WORKING WITH CODED DATA

To find the *average* of original data the average of coded data has to be *decoded* by reversing the procedure used in coding.

Example A

Average of coded data $= 0.4$

Average of original data $= 0.4 + 250 = 250.4$

Example B

Average of coded data $= 5.8$

Average of original data $= \dfrac{(5.8)}{1000} = .0058$

Example C

Average of coded data $= 5$

Average of original data $= \left(\dfrac{5}{1000}\right) + 1.24 = 1.245$

To find the range of original data, decoding is necessary only if we have multiplied the original data in coding.

Example A

Range of coded data $= (6 - (-4)) = 10$

Range of original data $= 10$

Because there was no multiplication in coding, the range of the original data is the same as that of the coded data.

Example B

Range of coded data $= (9 - 2) = 7$

Range of original data $= \dfrac{7}{1000} = 0.007$

Example C

Range of coded data $= (7 - 3) = 4$

Range of original data $= \dfrac{4}{1000} = 0.004$

Exercises

1. The data in Table 2.1 represent the fill weights of shaving cream in aerosol cans taken at the rate of five measurements every hour from a filling line. Calculate the X-bar and R for each of the hourly subgroups of five.

2. Calculate X-double bar, the average of the 10 hourly averages. We call this the grand average. Also calculate R-bar, the average of the 10 hourly ranges.

    (Answer: $\bar{\bar{X}} = 24.64$, $\bar{R} = 0.84$)

3. In computing control limits for the X-bar chart the following formulas are used:

    $$\text{UCL} = \bar{\bar{X}} + A_2\bar{R}$$
    $$\text{LCL} = \bar{\bar{X}} - A_2\bar{R}$$

    Use the values of $\bar{\bar{X}}$ and $\bar{R}$ from Problem 2 and calculate UCL and LCL, $A_2 = 0.577$

    (Answer: UCL $= 25.12$, LCL $= 24.16$)

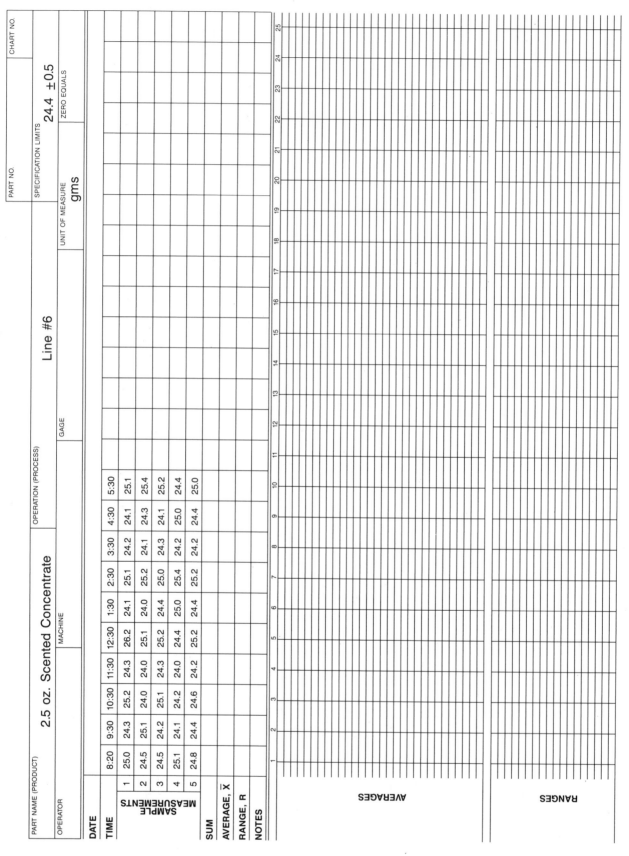

PART NAME (PRODUCT): 2.5 oz. Scented Concentrate

OPERATION (PROCESS): Line #6

PART NO.

SPECIFICATION LIMITS: 24.4 ±0.5

CHART NO.

OPERATOR

MACHINE

GAGE

UNIT OF MEASURE: gms

ZERO EQUALS

DATE

TIME	8:20	9:30	10:30	11:30	12:30	1:30	2:30	3:30	4:30	5:30
1	25.0	24.3	25.2	24.3	26.2	24.1	25.1	24.2	24.1	25.1
2	24.5	25.1	24.0	24.0	25.1	24.0	25.2	24.1	24.3	25.4
3	24.5	24.2	25.1	24.3	25.2	24.4	25.0	24.3	24.1	25.2
4	25.1	24.1	24.2	24.0	24.4	25.0	25.4	24.2	25.0	24.4
5	24.8	24.4	24.6	24.2	25.2	24.4	25.2	24.2	24.4	25.0

SAMPLE MEASUREMENTS

SUM

AVERAGE, $\bar{X}$

RANGE, R

NOTES

AVERAGES

RANGES

TABLE 2.1 VARIABLES CONTROL CHART ($\bar{X}$ AND R)

4. Calculate the values of U and L if:

$$\bar{p} = 0.2, n = 100$$

$$U = \bar{p} + 3\sqrt{\frac{\bar{p}(1 - \bar{p})}{n}}$$

$$L = \bar{p} - 3\sqrt{\frac{\bar{p}(1 - \bar{p})}{n}}$$

(Answer: U = 0.32, L = 0.08)

5. The following data represent the amount of perfume in grams shot into cans of antiperspirant. Code the data by first subtracting 1.0 and then by multiplying the result by 1000. Calculate the average and range of the data using the coded values:

   1.004   1.006   1.002   1.009   1.007

(Answer: $\bar{X}$ = 1.0056, R = 0.007)

REVIEW

Decimal addition
Decimal subtraction
Decimal multiplication
Decimal division
Average
Range
Squares
Square roots
Formula simplification
Coding

CHAPTER THREE: CONTROL CHARTS

In this chapter we will answer the following questions:

- What is a control chart?
- Why do we need control charts?

The details of designing and using control charts are covered in subsequent chapters.

CONCEPT OF CONTROL CHARTS

A control chart is a graph with a center line and two limit lines (Figure 3.1). Samples are drawn from the process at regular intervals and some measure of a quality characteristic, such as X-bar, R, etc., is computed and plotted on the chart. The limit lines provide the limit of variability in the measure due to natural causes of the process which should be expected and allowed for. Every process, be it an automatic lathe, a filling line, or a chemical reactor, produces some variability in the product characteristics due to variations in material, people, machinery, or environmental conditions.

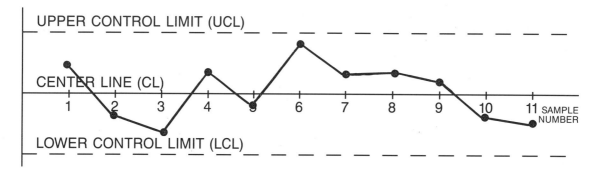

FIGURE 3.1 TYPICAL CONTROL CHART

We can find out from data collected from the process the amount of variability arising from the natural causes of the process. Then we can compute the limits to allow for this natural variability. We could use the control charts to continually reduce even this natural variability to as low a level as economically possible (Figure 3.2). Thus, there are two objectives in using control charts:

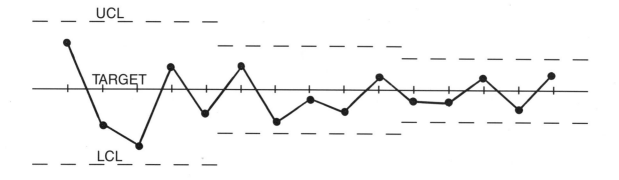

FIGURE 3.2 CONTINUOUS REDUCTION OF PROCESS VARIABILITY

16

1. To evaluate the current variability in the process and control the process to operate within this variability.

2. To improve the process continually by tracking down the sources of variability and reducing variability to the economic minimum level.

Dr. Walter Shewhart, who worked for Bell Laboratories in Princeton, New Jersey, during the mid-1920s, designed the control charts to achieve these objectives.

Since the control limits are designed to be the limits of natural variability, if the process is seen to produce measures within these limits we can conclude that the pattern of process variability is acceptable. Therefore, the process is *in-control*.

If any plotted measure falls outside the limits, we conclude that the pattern of process variability is unacceptable and the process is *not-in-control*. When the process is not-in-control it must be due to some extraneous cause that does not belong to the basic process: An *assignable cause* has entered the process. An assignable cause can be a broken tool, a loose nut, bad raw material, an untrained operator, or a tired inspector. When a sample produces an out-of-control measure, it is time to look for the cause and fix it.

The measure we plot on the chart depends on what we want to control in a process. If we want to control the average of a characteristic (e.g., the average net weight of sugar in a bag) we will be charting sample averages. We will then call this the average (X-bar) chart.

If we want to control the fraction of defectives produced in a process, we can plot the fraction of defectives in samples. This chart will be called the fraction defectives chart, or the p-chart. There are different charts to be used in different situations. These charts provide many benefits, some direct and some indirect.

BENEFITS FROM THE USE OF CONTROL CHARTS

1. Preventive Inspection and Corrective Action

   The control charts give timely signals when the process behaves abnormally so that the process can be corrected *before* it produces large quantities of defective products. They also help in continually improving the consistency of product quality.

2. Decisions Based on Facts Rather than Subjective Judgment

   Questions such as "What percent defectives?" "Which operator is consistent?" "Which process is capable?" can be answered with data, rather than by following intuition and subjective judgments.

   There have been many instances where "bad" machines considered to be incapable of holding tolerances have become good, capable machines once control charts were used. Subjective judgments can be erroneous.

3. Improved Inspection Methods

   Usually when a quality control program is installed, a review of inspection methods is conducted. People find they don't have the right instruments at the right place, or they find that labs take an inordinately long time for returning analyses. Such a review usually results in improved instrumentation and timely feedback of test results.

4. Improved Flow of Material

   When defectives are no longer made, there is less need for holding them for rework. When the control charts indicate that the products coming out are good, there is less need for holding finished products for inspection. Smoother product flow results.

5. Quality Consciousness

   Implementation of control charts serves as visible evidence of the company's commitment to quality. When successes are achieved in terms of avoidance of rejects and better quality products, others want to emulate the teams that achieved this success. There is a certain amount of satisfaction and pride in producing quality products. Everyone wants to jump on the bandwagon. There will be awareness of and desire for quality throughout the company.

6. Improved Product Quality/Customer Goodwill

   When product quality is good, there is no longer a need to push out low-grade goods to meet delivery. Customers have more confidence in the quality of the product. All this results in more new business.

7. Known Process Capability

   We should know which process is capable of meeting what specifications. Sometimes it is possible to improve process capability to meet a given specification. Sometimes it may not be economically possible. Then we may want to stay away from products we cannot make. In any case, it is good to know the capability of our processes.

8. Reduction in Scrap and Rework

   Often, it costs more to produce a defective product than a good product. Defective products use more material, machine time, and manpower. When these resources are used in making good products there is less waste, and therefore, more to sell. Productivity will also increase.

9. Effect on Manpower/Job Security

   A good quality control program, based on the concept of defect prevention, usually results in a better market position for the products and more business for the company. This means better staying power for the business and lasting jobs for its employees.

10. Avoidance of Over-Control

    Many processes have variability that is introduced because of adjustments made when it is not necessary. Control charts will tell us when a process must be adjusted and when it must be left alone. This alone usually results in savings worth the effort involved in making the control charts.

OPPORTUNITIES

SPC methods, as these control charts are called, can be used on any process, whether it produces a product or service (e.g., dry cleaning or parcel delivery). In any given plant, if we look around, there are always opportunities for quality improvement using SPC.

SPC methods have been used successfully by high-tech companies, smokestack companies, small companies, big companies, the Census Bureau, the U.S. military, and many others.

As Dr. W. Edwards Deming said, "Trouble is a common state of affairs in manufacturing." Thus, there are many opportunities to put statistical methods to use.

THREE TYPES OF CHARTS

Basically there are three types of control charts. They are listed as follows:

1. X-bar and R-charts
2. p-charts
3. c-charts

There are some variations of these charts. If we study these three basic types, others can be learned and used without much difficulty.

Where they are used, how they are used, how to calculate the control limits, etc., will be discussed in subsequent chapters.

REVIEW

A control chart is a device that tells you if the variability in a process is due to natural causes of the process and therefore should be left alone, or if it is due to extraneous causes and should be investigated.

Reduction in the amount of scrap and rework is the major benefit of control charts.

There are three basic types of control charts, with some variation.

CHAPTER FOUR: X-BAR AND R-CHARTS

When we want to control a quality characteristic that is a measurement, we use two control charts:

1. $\overline{X}$-chart (X-bar chart)
2. R-chart (range chart)

Together, these are known as the control charts for measurement (or variable). These charts would be used, for example, to control the amount of impurity in a chemical, the weight of sugar in a bag, the length of bolts, the strength of steel, etc. The method consists of taking subgroups of approximately five items at regular time intervals and computing the average ($\overline{X}$) and range (R) for each subgroup. The computed $\overline{X}$ values are plotted on a graph on which the limits for the $\overline{X}$s are drawn. This is the $\overline{X}$-chart. The R values are plotted on a graph wherein the limits for the Rs are drawn. This is the R-chart.

The process is said to be in-control if _both $\overline{X}$s and Rs_ are in-control. If either one of the charts shows out-of-control conditions, there is a problem. The reason must be found and an adjustment may be necessary.

Example

The process was a filling operation in a packaging plant that filled powder chemical into bags. The net weight of chemical in the bag was to be controlled. An inspector visited the process every two hours and selected five bags and weighed their contents and recorded the weights.

We will use a standard sheet as shown in Table 4.1A. All relevant information about the product and process should be recorded on this sheet, along with the data. This sheet also has room for calculating the $\overline{X}$ and R values, and for plotting the charts. The limits are calculated on the back of this sheet (Table 4.1B).

After the data are recorded as shown on the standard sheet, the following steps should be taken. We need about 25 subgroups to get started.

STEPS IN MAKING $\overline{X}$ AND R-CHARTS

Step 1

Compute $\overline{X}$ for each subgroup. (Round off all results to one decimal place beyond the number of decimal places in the observations.)

Step 2

Compute R for each subgroup.

Step 3

Compute $\overline{R}$ (R-bar, average of ranges). If there are K subgroups:

$$\overline{R} = \frac{\Sigma R}{K}$$

Step 4

Compute $\overline{\overline{X}}$ (X-double bar, average of the averages):

$$\overline{\overline{X}} = \frac{\Sigma \overline{X}}{K}$$

PART NAME (PRODUCT)		OPERATION (PROCESS)		CHART NO. 1/2
Bagged Chemical		Canning — Bldg. XYZ		PART NO. NO. 2½ bag

OPERATOR	MACHINE	GAGE	UNIT OF MEASURE	SPECIFICATION LIMITS	ZERO EQUALS
JOHN DOE	#01234	TOLEDO #446	LB		0 lb.

DATE	SEP 21				SEP 22				SEP 23				SEP 24					SEP 25			SEP 26			
TIME	9:30	10:50	11:45	2:30	8:05	10:00	1:15	5:00	9:30	1:15	1:45	3:30	8:20	10:25	11:30	2:30	19:20	11:40	2:00	3:00	7:30	8:35	10:40	4:30
1	22.0	20.5	20.0	21.0	22.5	23.0	19.0	21.5	21.0	21.5	20.0	19.0	19.5	20.0	22.5	21.5	19.0	21.0	20.0	22.0	19.0	21.5	22.5	22.5
2	22.5	22.5	20.5	22.0	19.5	23.5	20.0	20.5	22.5	23.0	19.5	21.0	20.5	21.5	19.5	20.5	21.5	20.5	23.5	20.5	20.5	25.0	22.0	22.0
3	22.5	22.5	23.0	22.0	22.5	21.0	22.0	19.0	20.0	22.0	21.0	21.0	21.0	24.0	21.0	22.0	23.0	19.5	24.0	21.0	21.0	21.0	23.0	22.0
4	24.0	23.0	22.0	23.0	22.0	22.0	20.5	19.5	22.0	23.0	20.0	21.0	20.5	23.0	21.5	21.5	21.0	22.0	20.5	22.5	20.5	18.0	22.0	19.5
5	23.5	21.5	21.5	22.0	21.0	20.0	22.5	19.5	22.0	18.5	20.5	20.5	21.0	20.0	21.0	23.5	23.5	21.0	21.5	20.0	22.5	21.0	23.5	20.5
SUM																								
AVERAGE, X̄	22.9	22.0	21.4	22.0	21.5	21.9	20.8	20.0	21.5	21.6	20.2	20.5	20.5	21.7	21.1	21.8	21.6	20.8	21.9	21.2	20.7	21.3	22.6	21.3
RANGE, R	2.0	2.5	3.0	2.0	3.0	3.5	3.5	2.5	2.5	4.5	1.5	2.0	1.5	4.0	3.0	3.0	4.5	2.5	4.0	2.5	3.5	7.0	1.5	3.0
NOTES																								

$UCL_{\bar{X}} = 23.11$

$\bar{\bar{X}} = 21.37$

$LCL_{\bar{X}} = 19.63$

$UCL = 6.38$

$\bar{R} = 3.02$

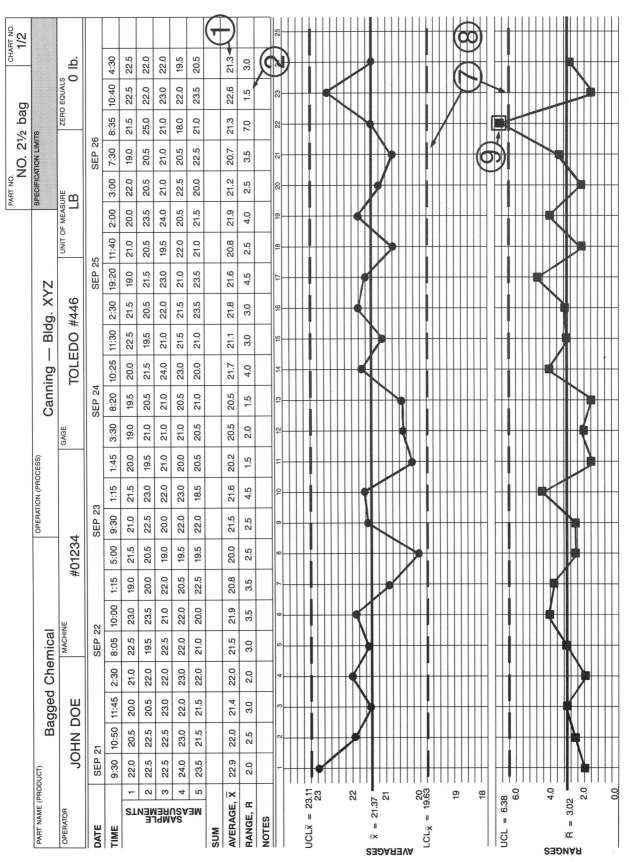

TABLE 4.1A VARIABLES CONTROL CHART ($\bar{X}$ AND R)

Product: #2 Chemical   **Machine:** Bldg XYZ   **Calculated by:** 7D

$$\overline{\overline{X}} = \Sigma\,\overline{X}\,/\,k = \underline{\quad 512.8 \quad} \Big/ \underline{\quad\quad 24 \quad\quad} = \underline{21.37}$$
$$\text{(Sum of all } \overline{X}\text{s)} \quad \text{(Number of } \overline{X}\text{s added)}$$

④

$$\overline{R} = \Sigma\,R\,/\,k = \underline{\quad 72.5 \quad} \Big/ \underline{\quad\quad 24 \quad\quad} = \underline{3.02}$$
$$\text{(Sum of all Rs)} \quad \text{(Number of Rs added)}$$

③

Subgroup size: n = $\underline{5}$ Target (if given) = $\underline{\text{none}}$

In the formulas for limits use values of D_3, D_4, and A_2 from the table below based on subgroup size. Use $\overline{X}$ = Target, if one is available. Otherwise use the value computed above.

Limits for R-Chart:

$$UCL(R) = D_4\overline{R} = \underset{(D_4)}{\underline{2.114}} \times \underset{(\overline{R})}{\underline{3.02}} = \underline{6.38}$$

$$CL(R) \;\;= \overline{R} \;\;\;= \underline{3.02}$$

$$LCL(R) = D_3\overline{R} = \underset{(D_3)}{\underline{0}} \times \underset{(\overline{R})}{\underline{3.02}} = \underline{0.0}$$

⑤

Limits for $\overline{X}$-Chart:

$$UCL\,(\overline{X}) = \overline{\overline{X}} + A_2\overline{R} = \underset{(\overline{X})}{\underline{21.37}} + \underset{(A_2)}{\underline{0.577}} \times \underset{(\overline{R})}{\underline{3.02}} = \underline{23.11}$$

$$CL(\overline{X}) \;\;= \overline{\overline{X}} \;\;\;\;\;\;= \underline{21.37}$$

$$LCL(\overline{X}) \;\;= \overline{\overline{X}} - A_2\overline{R} = \underset{(\overline{X})}{\underline{21.37}} - \underset{(A_2)}{\underline{0.577}} \times \underset{(\overline{R})}{\underline{3.02}} = \underline{19.63}$$

⑥

Factors for control chart limit:

Subgroup size (n)	D_3	D_4	A_2	d_2
2	0	3.268	1.880	1.128
3	0	2.574	1.023	1.693
4	0	2.282	0.729	2.059
5	0	2.114	0.577	2.326
6	0	2.004	0.483	2.534
7	0.076	1.924	0.419	2.704
8	0.136	1.864	0.373	2.847
9	0.184	1.816	0.337	2.970
10	0.223	1.777	0.308	3.078

TABLE 4.1B CALCULATION OF CONTROL LIMITS FOR X-BAR AND R-CHARTS

Step 5

Compute the control limits for the R-chart using the following formulas:

$$UCL\ (R) = D_4\overline{R}$$
$$CL\ (R) = \overline{R}$$
$$LCL\ (R) = D_3\overline{R}$$

The factors D_3 and D_4 are available from standard tables. One such table is shown in Table 4.1B. D_3 and D_4 must be chosen based on subgroup size (the number of items in a subgroup). $D_3 = 0$ for subgroup sizes of six or less. Thus, the LCL (R) is zero for subgroups of sizes six or less.

Step 6

Compute the control limits for $\overline{X}$-chart using the following formulas:

$$UCL\ (\overline{X}) = \overline{\overline{X}} + A_2\overline{R}$$
$$CL\ (\overline{X}) = \overline{\overline{X}}$$
$$LCL\ (\overline{X}) = \overline{\overline{X}} - A_2\overline{R}$$

The factor A_2 must be chosen based on the subgroup size from the table.

Step 7

Select a proper scale and draw the center line and limit lines for the $\overline{X}$-chart and R-chart. Select the scale so that the charts do not become too narrow. Draw CLs as solid lines and limit lines as broken lines.

Step 8

Plot the $\overline{X}$ values on the $\overline{X}$-chart and R values on the R-chart. Plot $\overline{X}$ values with a large dot (●). Plot R values with an "x" or a box (□). Join the plotted points with straight lines.

Step 9

If any of the values are outside the limits on either one of the charts, the process is not-in-control. Mark the values outside the limits with a large circle (○).

Step 10

If the process is in-control, do not make any adjustment to the process. If the process is not-in-control, the reason for this should be discovered. If points are outside limits on the $\overline{X}$-chart, it means the process average has changed. If points on the R chart are outside limits, the process variability has changed.

To discover the assignable cause that is throwing the process out-of-control, we need to use our knowledge of the process. Often the reasons for trouble are obvious and can be repaired easily. Sometimes the causes are not apparent and a specialist or quality engineer may need to be called in.

Step 11

If the process is in-control, the control limits calculated previously can be used for future control. (You will not find many processes in-control if they have not been previously controlled using control charts.) If the process was not-in-control and subsequently adjusted, the out-of-control points can be thrown out and new limits figured with the remaining data. These new limits can be used in the future.

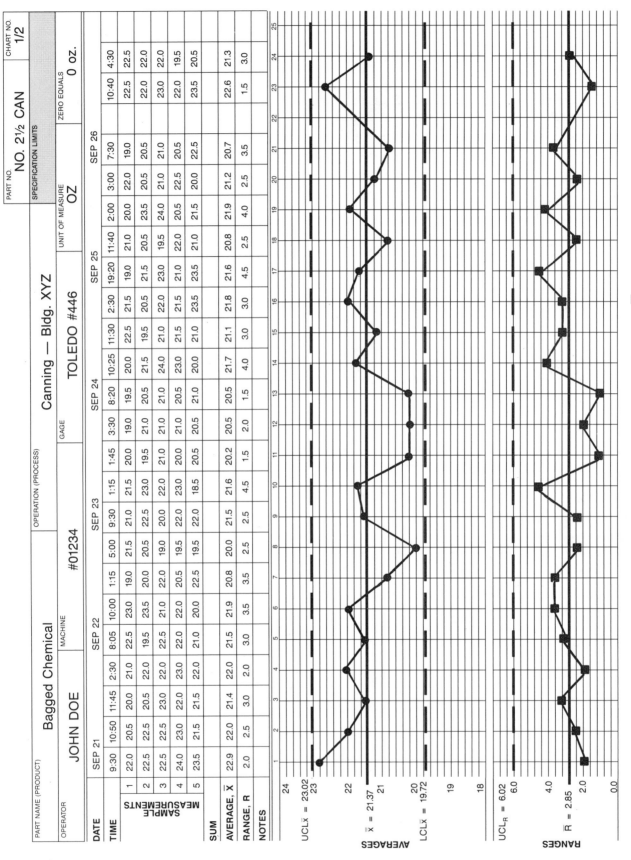

TABLE 4.2 VARIABLES CONTROL CHART (X̄ AND R)

PART NAME (PRODUCT)	OPERATION (PROCESS)	PART NO. NO. 2½ CAN	CHART NO. 1/2
Bagged Chemical	Canning — Bldg. XYZ	SPECIFICATION LIMITS	ZERO EQUALS 0 oz.
OPERATOR: JOHN DOE	MACHINE: #01234	GAGE: TOLEDO #446	UNIT OF MEASURE: OZ

DATE	SEP 21				SEP 22				SEP 23				SEP 24				SEP 25				SEP 26		
TIME	9:30	10:50	11:45	2:30	8:05	10:00	1:15	5:00	9:30	1:15	1:45	3:30	8:20	10:25	11:30	2:30	19:20	11:40	2:00	3:00	7:30	10:40	4:30
1	22.0	20.5	20.0	21.0	22.5	23.0	19.0	21.5	21.0	21.5	20.0	19.0	19.5	20.0	22.5	21.5	19.0	21.0	20.0	22.0	19.0	22.5	22.5
2	22.5	22.5	20.5	22.0	19.5	23.5	20.0	20.5	22.5	23.0	19.5	21.0	20.5	21.5	19.5	20.5	21.5	20.5	23.5	20.5	20.5	22.0	22.0
3	22.5	22.5	23.0	22.0	22.5	21.0	22.0	19.0	20.0	22.0	21.0	21.0	21.0	24.0	21.0	22.0	23.0	19.5	24.0	21.0	21.0	23.0	22.0
4	24.0	23.0	22.0	23.0	22.0	22.0	20.5	19.5	22.0	23.0	20.0	21.0	20.5	23.0	21.5	21.5	21.0	22.0	20.5	22.5	20.5	22.0	19.5
5	23.5	21.5	21.5	22.0	21.0	20.0	22.5	19.5	22.0	18.5	20.5	20.5	21.0	20.0	21.0	23.5	23.5	21.0	21.5	20.0	22.5	23.5	20.5
SUM																							
AVERAGE, X̄	22.9	22.0	21.4	22.0	21.5	21.9	20.8	20.0	21.5	21.6	20.2	20.5	20.5	21.7	21.1	21.8	21.6	20.8	21.9	21.2	20.7	22.6	21.3
RANGE, R	2.0	2.5	3.0	2.0	3.0	3.5	3.5	2.5	2.5	4.5	1.5	2.0	1.5	4.0	3.0	3.0	4.5	2.5	4.0	2.5	3.5	1.5	3.0
NOTES																							

AVERAGES:
UCLx̄ = 23.02
x̄̄ = 21.37
LCLx̄ = 19.72

RANGES:
UCLR = 6.02
R̄ = 2.85

CHART NO.

PART NO.

PART NAME (PRODUCT): 2.5 oz. Scented . . .

SPECIFICATION LIMITS: 24.4 ± 0.5

ZERO EQUALS: 0 gm.

OPERATION (PROCESS): Filler #7

OPERATOR: S.M.

MACHINE

GAGE

UNIT OF MEASURE

DATE: 7/28/86 ... 7/29

	8:00	9:00	10	11	12	13	14	15	16	17	18	19	20	21	22	8 A	9	10	11	12
1	25.0	24.3	25.2	24.3	26.2	24.1	25.1	24.2	24.1	25.1	24.6	23.9	25.1	24.8	24.4	23.9	24.5	24.4	25.2	23.1
2	24.5	25.1	24.0	24.0	25.1	24.0	25.2	24.1	24.3	25.4	24.9	23.7	27.3	24.4	24.3	23.4	24.8	24.5	25.6	23.2
3	24.5	24.2	25.1	24.3	25.2	24.4	25.0	24.3	24.1	25.2	24.1	24.2	27.3	24.1	24.9	23.8	24.8	24.8	25.3	23.4
4	25.1	24.1	24.2	24.0	24.4	25.0	25.4	24.2	25.0	24.4	24.0	24.1	27.1	24.3	25.0	24.0	24.9	24.6	25.2	23.4
5																				

SAMPLE MEASUREMENTS — SUM, AVERAGE X̄, RANGE R, NOTES

AVERAGES

RANGES

TABLE 4.3A VARIABLES CONTROL CHART (X̄ AND R)

Product: **Machine:**   **Calculated by:**

$\overline{\overline{X}} = \Sigma \overline{X} / k = $ _____ / _____ = ____
                         (Sum of all $\overline{X}$s)   (Number of $\overline{X}$s added)

$\overline{R} = \Sigma R / k = $ _____ / _____ = ____
                      (Sum of all Rs)   (Number of Rs added)

Subgroup size: n = ____   Target (if given) = ____

In the formulas for limits use values of D_3, D_4, and A_2 from the table below based on subgroup size. Use $\overline{X}$ = Target, if one is available. Otherwise use the value computed above.

Limits for R-Chart:

$UCL(R) = D_4\overline{R} = $ ____ $\times$ ____ = ____
                 (D₄)   ($\overline{R}$)

$CL(R) = \overline{R} = $ ____

$LCL(R) = D_3\overline{R} = $ ___ $\times$ ___ = __
              (D₃)   ($\overline{R}$)

Limits for $\overline{X}$-Chart:

$UCL(\overline{X}) = \overline{\overline{X}} + A_2\overline{R} = $ ____ + ____ $\times$ ___ = ____
                       ($\overline{X}$)   (A₂)   ($\overline{R}$)

$CL(\overline{X}) = \overline{\overline{X}} = $ ____

$LCL(\overline{X}) = \overline{\overline{X}} - A_2\overline{R} = $ ___ $-$ ___ $\times$ ___ = ____
                      ($\overline{X}$)   (A₂)   ($\overline{R}$)

Factors for control chart limit:

Subgroup size (n)	D_3	D_4	A_2	d_2
2	0	3.268	1.880	1.128
3	0	2.574	1.023	1.693
4	0	2.282	0.729	2.059
5	0	2.114	0.577	2.326
6	0	2.004	0.483	2.534
7	0.076	1.924	0.419	2.704
8	0.136	1.864	0.373	2.847
9	0.184	1.816	0.337	2.970
10	0.223	1.777	0.308	3.078

TABLE 4.3B   CALCULATION OF CONTROL LIMITS FOR X-BAR AND R-CHARTS

Example

Sample number 22 is thrown out (assuming the process was properly adjusted) and new limits are calculated. We find all $\overline{X}$ and R values are within these new limits. (See Table 4.2 which shows the new control limits with the in-control data.) These limits can be used in the future.

Exercise

The data shown in Table 4.3A are the weights of concentrate in 2.5-oz scented deodorant cans filled on a filling line. There are 20 subgroups of four observations each. Calculate $\overline{X}$ and R values for each subgroup, and the control limits for both $\overline{X}$ and R charts. If the filling process is not-in-control, take out the points outside the limits and recalculate the limits for future use.

(Answer: Using $\overline{\overline{X}}$ = 24.4 the given target, limits for future control are:

$$\text{UCL } (\overline{X}) = 24.87 \qquad \text{UCL } (R) = 1.46$$
$$\text{LCL } (\overline{X}) = 23.93 \qquad \text{LCL } (R) = 0 \qquad)$$

SOME NOTES ABOUT X-BAR AND R-CHARTS

1. Of all the statistical quality control methods, X-bar and R-charts are the most useful and popular tools.

2. X-bar and R-charts can be used for many purposes:

   - To control a process so that it produces consistent quality
   - To avoid over-control
   - To study process capability
   - To improve process capability
   - To be an acceptance tool

3. The control charts do not improve processes. We improve the processes with the help of control charts.

4. The situations in which control charts are to be used and the variable to be charted should be decided according to established priorities. Usually process control teams that include line personnel select the situations in which control charts are to be used and the variables to be controlled. Use of control charts should start with the most important or the most troublesome variable(s). Do not use any more control charts than absolutely necessary.

5. Typically, the *frequency of sampling* will be high in the beginning stages of control chart use. The frequency can be reduced as the confidence in the stability of the process improves. The control chart can be discontinued if it seems to have served its purpose.

6. *Subgroup sizes* of four or five are preferred for theoretical reasons. However, if the situation demands, other sizes from two to 10 can be used. The R-chart becomes unreliable with larger sample sizes.

7. Before starting charts, make certain the instruments, scales, and gages are properly calibrated. If not, the proper authorities should be notified and the situation remedied.

8. In the case of the X-bar chart, instead of using $\overline{\overline{X}}$ for the center line, we can use a *given standard value* or "target" for process average.

    There are process characteristics that can be easily controlled to a given average value. Cutting labels to a given width, filling bags with sugar to a given weight, and punching holes at given centers are examples of such "tweakable" processes. For such processes it might be a good idea to use the target as the center of the X-bar chart.

    There are also process characteristics that cannot be "tweaked" to any given average. The amount of impurity in a chemical, the strength of plastic, and the density of color in a printing process are examples of process characteristics that must first be controlled at their "current" average using $\overline{X}$ at the center of the X-bar chart. Then over a period of time effort must be made to move the average in the desired direction.

9. *Subgrouping* refers to the way observations are grouped in a subgroup. Subgrouping should be done in such a way that it would provide leads to discover the assignable cause when the process is not-in-control. Two examples are used to illustrate this idea.

Example A

A milling machine with two heads was cutting an important key-way. The key-way width was controlled by control charts. Subgroups of five measurements were taken every hour from the total production of the machine. The control chart showed that the process was going out-of-control periodically.

Next, it was decided that subgroups of five would be taken alternately from each head. That is, if the subgroup at 8:00 am came from the first head, the subgroup at 9:00 am would come from the second head. It soon became clear that the second head was the culprit as the $\overline{X}$ values from that head were periodically outside limits. It was found to have a fixture that was loosening over time. A lock nut solved the problem. Further control charting for the milling machine used subgroups based on a head.

Example B

A filler that filled liquid detergent in bottles on an automatic filling line had 18 heads. Each head could lose its adjustment, be clogged, or in some way be affected by assignable causes. The amount of liquid in a bottle had to be controlled using an X-bar chart.

One way to subgroup was to take five bottles every hour at the end of the line, regardless of which head filled the bottles. Such a subgrouping would be alright as long as the process was in-control. When it went out-of-control, we could not see which head needed fixing unless we did further experimentation on all 18 heads.

An alternate method of subgrouping was to take five bottles from each head each hour, which would tell which head was wrong. This was a very expensive way of subgrouping because so many checks were needed per hour.

We decided to take 18 checks per hour, one from each head. Subgrouping was done by putting bottles from the first six heads in subgroup 1, bottles from the next six heads in subgroup 2, and bottles from the last six heads in subgroup 3. If an $\overline{X}$ value was to fall outside limits, we would know which group of heads needed to be checked. This was a good compromise between the two previous alternatives and worked well.

Such *rational subgrouping* should be used to discover assignable causes. Proper subgrouping helps to get the most out of control charts.

10. *Control limits are different from specification limits.* They should not be confused with each other. Control limits in the X-bar chart are limits for the averages, whereas specification limits are limits for the individual values. The averages have smaller variability in them than the individual values. (Compare the variability in the individual values of the first two samples with that of the averages of the same samples in Figure 4.1.) Because the variability in averages is smaller than the variability in individuals, the limits for averages will be narrower than the limits for individuals.

    Thus, if we compare the averages with the specification limits we will almost always find the averages falling inside specification limits. Similarly, if we compare the individuals with the limits for the averages, the individual values will often fall outside these limits. Both situations will give erroneous signals. As a rule, *it is a good idea not to draw specification limits on control charts* to avoid confusion.

11. For people who are accustomed to adjusting processes after comparing individual values to specification limits, it is difficult to learn this new lesson: Adjust the process only when an average value is outside the control limits. The averages will discover changes in the process more quickly than the individual values because the averages are clouded by less noise (variability) compared to the individuals. Adjustments based on individuals lead to over-control.

12. Can a process be in-control and yet produce products that are out of specification? Yes, it can happen, especially in the early stages of controlling a process. Remember that we use an estimate of natural variability in the process to design control limits. This means the control chart tries to hold the process within its natural variability. If this natural variability is too large compared to what is allowed by the specifications, there may be out-of-specification items even when the process is in-control. This is when we will analyze the sources of the natural variability and try to eliminate as much of it as possible. Such a study is part of what is known as a process capability study.

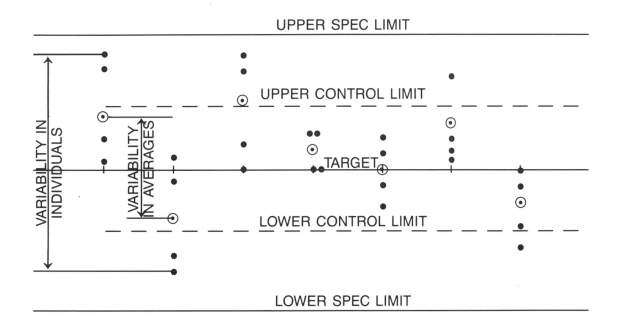

FIGURE 4.1 VARIABILITY IN AVERAGES IS SMALLER THAN IN INDIVIDUALS

Furthermore, if a process is not being controlled or cannot be controlled with the target at the center of the chart, the natural center of the process may be different from the center of the specification. In such cases the process could be producing out-of-specification items even though the process is stable. Again, a capability study will reveal this condition and will point to remedial action.

A process can also be out-of-control and produce products that are within specification if the specifications are loose and there is room for the process to fluctuate. This will indicate that the specifications are set with no relation to the capability of the process.

After discussing the two situations, it may become clear why we have to make a capability study — studying the ability of the process to meet the required specifications — on a process after it has been brought in-control. The details of making a capability study, and the methods of measuring the capability of a process will be discussed in a later chapter.

13. Thus far, we have mentioned only one rule to determine when a process is in-control and when it is not-in-control: A process is not-in-control when one $\bar{X}$ or R value falls outside a control limit; otherwise a process is in-control. There are other rules that can be used to discover the presence of assignable causes even before an $\bar{X}$ or R value falls outside the limits. Some of these rules reveal potential problems. There are several rules available; we will use just two of them:

   • Runs above and below the center line
   • Runs up and down

Runs Above and Below the Center Line

When consecutive points on a control chart fall on the same side of the center line, we have runs above or below the center line. The number of consecutive points in a run is called the length of the run. Figure 4.2 shows some examples of runs.

One rule to remember with runs is that the process should be considered out-of-control if there is a run of length seven or more on the same side of the center line.

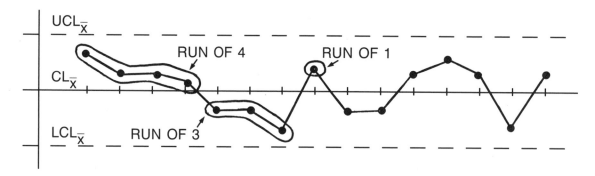

FIGURE 4.2 RUNS ABOVE AND BELOW CENTER LINE

Runs Up and Down

When consecutive points fall continuously in an increasing or decreasing direction, we have runs up or down. Runs up or down indicate trends in the charted values. Figure 4.3 shows some examples of runs up and down. With runs up and down, a process should be considered out-of-control if there is a run up or run down of length seven or more. In counting runs up or down include values both above and below the center line. Runs up and down are good indicators of where the process is going, especially with processes that deteriorate slowly over time.

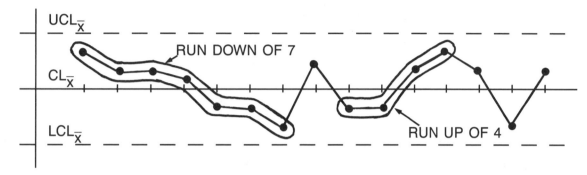

FIGURE 4.3 RUNS UP AND DOWN

REVIEW

Two charts are needed to control measurements:

1. X-bar chart (average chart)
2. R-chart (range chart)

Approximately 25 subgroups of about five measurements are needed to start the charts. Limits are calculated as follows:

$$UCL\ (\overline{X}) = \overline{\overline{X}} + A_2\overline{R}$$
$$CL\ (\overline{X}) = \overline{\overline{X}}$$
$$LCL\ (\overline{X}) = \overline{\overline{X}} - A_2\overline{R}$$

$$UCL\ (R) = D_4\overline{R}$$
$$CL\ (R) = \overline{R}$$
$$LCL\ (R) = D_3\overline{R}$$

The standard sheet should be used to fill in relevant information about the process.

Use the rules for plotting and charting.

Check instruments and gages for calibration before starting charts.

Use proper subgrouping to get the most out of control charts.

Use the run-of-seven rule. Use runs up and down for trends.

Do not put specification limits on X-bar charts.

CHAPTER FIVE: ATTRIBUTE CONTROL CHARTS

There are two types of control charts used with attribute data:

1. p-chart (fraction defective chart)
2. c-chart (defects per unit chart)

Note the difference between "defective" and a "defect." A defective item may have more than one defect; a defect may or may not make an item defective.

THE p-CHART

The p-chart is used to control the level of defectives produced by a process. It is used with attribute inspection where products are classified as good/bad, clean/unclean, tight/loose, etc., and no measurements are recorded. This chart would be appropriate to use where there is a large quantity produced and a certain amount of defectives is unavoidable. However, the proportion of defectives should be watched, controlled, and reduced.

For example, this chart could be used to control the proportion of bottles with bad litho or to control the proportion of forgings with surface defects. Here again, the major value of the control chart lies not so much in its ability to control the proportion defectives at the "current" value, but in its usefulness in reducing the proportion defectives to the minimum possible level. This procedure is described in the following steps.

Step 1

Collect the data. Take subgroups of 20 to 200 items (subgroup sizes are usually large for this chart and can even be larger than 200) at regular time intervals such as every hour or every two hours. The subgroup size and the frequency of sampling should be decided based on the rate of production and the cost and time needed for inspection. Inspect each subgroup, count the number of defectives in each, and write down the counts on a standard sheet.

Step 2

Calculate the fraction defectives (p's) in each subgroup using the following formula:

$$p = \frac{\text{number of defectives in the subgroup}}{\text{total number of items in the subgroup}}$$

(round p values to the nearest hundredth)

Step 3

Calculate the average fraction defective (p-bar) after inspecting approximately 25 subgroups:

$$\bar{p} = \frac{\Sigma p}{K}$$

where K is the number of subgroups inspected.
(round the $\bar{p}$ value to the nearest thousandth)

Step 4

Calculate the control limits using the following formulas:

$$\text{UCL (p)} = \bar{p} + 3\sqrt{\frac{\bar{p}(1 - \bar{p})}{n}}$$

$$\text{CL (p)} = \bar{p}$$

$$\text{LCL (p)} = \bar{p} - 3\sqrt{\frac{\bar{p}(1 - \bar{p})}{n}}$$

where n is the number of items in each subgroup.
(round the limits to the nearest thousandth)

Step 5

Draw the control limits and the center line on the graph paper portion of the standard sheet using a suitable scale.

Step 6

Plot the fraction defectives (p values) corresponding to each subgroup on the graph where the control lines have already been drawn.

Step 7

Interpret the chart. If all the plotted p values are within limits, the process is in-control; otherwise the assignable cause must be investigated and removed.

Example

The process was a single spindle automatic lathe that produced wood screws. The screws were checked for several defects such as length (using a gage), slot position, finish, etc., and were classified as good or defective.

Step 1. Collect the data. Fifty screws were taken every half hour and the screws were inspected and the number of defectives in each subgroup was recorded as shown in Table 5.1.

Step 2. Calculate the p's. The fraction defectives were calculated for each subgroup. For example, for subgroup 1:

$$p = \frac{1}{50} = 0.02$$

Step 3. Compute $\bar{p}$, average of the p's:

$$\bar{p} = \frac{(0.02 + 0.04 + ... + 0.02 + 0.00)}{25}$$

$$= \frac{0.68}{25} = 0.027$$

Product number: 176 Woodscrew					Machine number: 743 Auto Lathe					Date:									Inspector: KT					

Defect category: Length, slot, finish								Gage used: Go-no go					Subgroup size: n = 50												

Subgroup number	1	2	3	4	5	6	7	8	9	10	11	12	13	14	15	16	17	18	19	20	21	22	23	24	25
Number of defectives	1	2	5	6	3	5	2	1	1	0	0	1	0	1	0	2	1	0	0	1	1	0	0	1	0
Fraction defectives, p	.02	.04	.10	.12	.06	.10	.04	.02	.02	0	0	.02	0	.02	0	.04	.02	0	0	.02	.02	0	0	.02	0

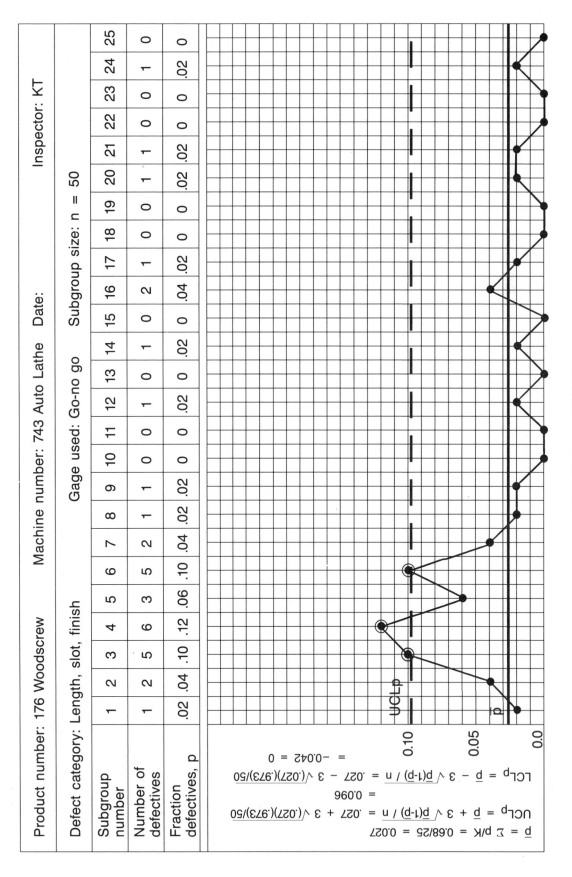

$$\bar{p} = \Sigma\, p/k = 0.68/25 = 0.027$$

$$UCL_p = \bar{p} + 3\sqrt{\bar{p}(1-\bar{p})/n} = .027 + 3\sqrt{(.027)(.973)/50}$$
$$= 0.096$$

$$LCL_p = \bar{p} - 3\sqrt{\bar{p}(1-\bar{p})/n} = .027 - 3\sqrt{(.027)(.973)/50}$$
$$= -0.042 = 0$$

0.10   0.05   0.0

UCLp

p̄

TABLE 5.1 p-CHART

Step 4. Compute the control limits:

$$UCL\ (p) = \bar{p} + 3\sqrt{\frac{\bar{p}(1 - \bar{p})}{n}}$$

$$= 0.027 + 3\sqrt{\frac{(0.027)\ (0.973)}{50}}$$

$$= 0.096$$

$$CL\ (p) = 0.027$$

$$LCL\ (p) = \bar{p} - 3\sqrt{\frac{\bar{p}(1 - \bar{p})}{n}}$$

$$= 0.027 - 3\sqrt{\frac{(0.027)\ (0.973)}{50}}$$

$$= -0.042 = 0.00$$

Note that if we get a negative number for the LCL of a p-chart we will make it zero.

Step 5. Draw the control limits (Table 5.1).

Step 6. Plot the p values (Table 5.1).

Step 7. Interpret the chart. The process is not in-control. Several p values are outside limit and need to be investigated.

It is possible to remove those p values outside the limits and recalculate the limits from the remaining data for future use, provided the causes resulting in the out-of-control condition have been found and removed.

In the example, the out-of-control points had been obtained during start-up and the process stabilized at a lower average fraction defective after start-up. Thus, we could remove the three p values corresponding to sample numbers 3, 4, and 6.

$$new\ \bar{p} = \frac{0.36}{22} = 0.016$$

The new limits are:

$$UCL\ (p) = 0.016 + 3\sqrt{\frac{(.016)\ (.984)}{50}}$$

$$= 0.069$$

$$CL\ (p) = 0.016$$

$$LCL\ (p) = 0.016 - 3\sqrt{\frac{(.016)\ (.984)}{50}}$$

$$= -.037 = 0$$

All the "remaining" p values are within these limits. These limits can be used for future control of the process.

Exercise

The data in Table 5.2 come from an inspection station at the end of a packaging line where filled bottles are inspected for cleanliness, label position, correct valve orientation, printed code, etc., and are classified as good or bad. Subgroups of 20 bottles were taken every half hour and the number of bad bottles in each subgroup was recorded. Using a p-chart, verify if the filling operation is in-control with regard to the defects checked.

(Answer: UCL (p) = 0.219, LCL (p) = 0; process is in-control)

THE c-CHART

The c-chart is used where the quality of products is controlled by controlling the number of defects per unit. A certain number of defects may be tolerable, but the number of defects per unit should be watched, controlled, and reduced.

For example, a certain number of knots (defects) per each 4 foot by 8 foot sheet of plywood may be tolerable, but this number needs to be controlled. Another example is to control the quality of printing by controlling the number of errors (overexposure/underexposure, smudges, etc.) per printed sheet.

The procedure for using the c-chart is explained in the following steps:

Step 1

Collect the data. Choose a unit at regular time intervals — for example, every hour or every two hours. Inspect the units and count the number of defects in each unit and write down the counts on a standard sheet as shown in Table 5.3. These counts are the c values.

Step 2

Calculate $\bar{c}$. After inspecting approximately 25 units, calculate the average defects per unit using the formula:

$$\bar{c} = \frac{\Sigma c}{K}$$

where K is the number of units inspected.
(round c to the nearest tenth)

Step 3

Calculate the control limits using the following formulas:

$$UCL\ (c) = \bar{c} + 3\sqrt{\bar{c}}$$

$$CL\ (c) = \bar{c}$$

$$LCL\ (c) = \bar{c} - 3\sqrt{\bar{c}}$$

(round the limits to the nearest tenth)

Step 4

Draw the control limits and center line on the graph paper portion of the standard sheet using suitable scale.

Step 5

Plot all c values on the graph.

Product number: Starch Machine number: Line #5 Date: Inspector: KSK

Defect category: Appearance / Cleanliness

Gage used:

Subgroup size:

Subgroup number	1 830	2 930	3 1030	4 1130	5	6	7	8	9	10	11	12	13	14	15	16	17	18	19	20	21	22	23	24	25
Number of defectives	0	0	4	3	2	0	1	2	0	3	0	4	1	1	1	2	1	0	0	1	1	0	2	1	0
Fraction defectives, p																									

$$\bar{p} = \Sigma p/k = \quad / \quad =$$

$$UCL_p = \bar{p} + 3\sqrt{\bar{p}(1-\bar{p})/n} =$$

$$LCL_p = \bar{p} - 3\sqrt{\bar{p}(1-\bar{p})/n} =$$

TABLE 5.2 p-CHART

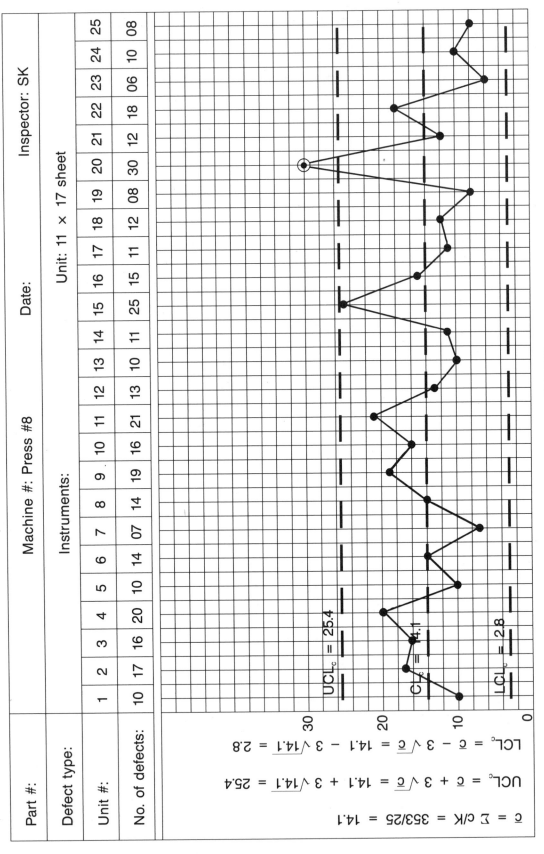

Part #:		Machine #: Press #8								Date:									Inspector: SK						
Defect type:																									
		Instruments:													Unit: 11 × 17 sheet										
Unit #:	1	2	3	4	5	6	7	8	9	10	11	12	13	14	15	16	17	18	19	20	21	22	23	24	25
No. of defects:	10	17	16	20	10	14	07	14	19	16	21	13	10	11	25	15	11	12	08	30	12	18	06	10	08

$$\bar{c} = \Sigma\, c/k = 353/25 = 14.1$$

$$UCL_c = \bar{c} + 3\sqrt{\bar{c}} = 14.1 + 3\sqrt{14.1} = 25.4$$

$$LCL_c = \bar{c} - 3\sqrt{\bar{c}} = 14.1 - 3\sqrt{14.1} = 2.8$$

TABLE 5.3 c-CHART

38

Step 6

Interpret the chart. If all the plotted c values are within limits, the process is in-control. Otherwise the cause for the trouble must be investigated and corrective action taken.

Example

A laminating press was putting a plastic lamination on 11 inch by 17 inch printed pieces of artwork, which were later cut into luggage tags. Chicken scratches were showing up on the sheets and were controlled using a c-chart.

Step 1. Collect the data. One sheet was pulled out every half hour and an inspector counted the number of scratches per sheet and wrote them down on a standard sheet as shown in Table 5.3.

Step 2. Calculate $\bar{c}$:

$$\bar{c} = \frac{353}{25} = 14.1$$

Step 3. Calculate the limits:

$$\text{UCL (c)} = 14.1 + 3\sqrt{14.1} = 25.4$$
$$\text{CL (c)} = 14.1$$
$$\text{LCL (c)} = 14.1 - 3\sqrt{14.1} = 2.8$$

Step 4. Draw control limits (Table 5.3).

Step 5. Plot the c values (Table 5.3).

Step 6. Read the chart. The process was not in-control. The number of chicken scratches on some sheets was too many when compared with others. The reason for this needed to be investigated.

The chicken scratches were caused by several factors: temperature and surface condition of the platen, pressure applied, quality of the plastic material, and atmospheric conditions, to name a few. The collection of data for the c-chart enabled discovery of a few abnormal conditions that produced out-of-control data. It also brought out the need for further investigation as the average number of scratches per sheet was high and was responsible for a high scrap rate.

An experiment was conducted to discover the optimal pressure and temperature of the press. A specialist in plastic technology was brought in to help with the investigation. Several remedies were applied and the process improved considerably.

This is an example where the assignable cause was not obvious and some investigation was required. It proved the saying that "statistical quality control is 10 percent statistics and 90 percent engineering."

It is possible, as in other charts, to remove the out-of-control points from the data (assuming the causes have been rectified) and recalculate the limits for future use.

For the example at the current stage of control, sample 20 can be removed and new limits calculated as follows:

$$\text{new } \bar{c} = \frac{323}{24} = 13.5$$

New limits would be:

$$\text{UCL (c)} = 13.5 + 3\sqrt{13.5} = 24.5$$
$$\text{CL (c)} = 13.5$$
$$\text{LCL (c)} = 13.5 - 3\sqrt{13.5} = 2.5$$

Now unit 15 is seen outside these limits. If we remove this sample:

$$\text{new } \bar{c} = \frac{298}{23} = 13.0$$

New limits would be:

$$\text{UCL (c)} = 13.0 + 3\sqrt{13.0} = 23.8$$
$$\text{CL (c)} = 13.0$$
$$\text{LCL (c)} = 13.0 - 3\sqrt{13.0} = 2.2$$

The remaining c values are within these limits and these can be used for the next stage of process control.

This method of calculating control limits for future use does not always need to be followed. In a situation where the process is badly out-of-control and several assignable causes are discovered and removed, the first set of data may have no relevance to the future process. In that case we can take a new set of data from the "new" process and design limits for future use.

Where data are expensive or when it takes a long time to gather a new set of 25 samples, we can use the above procedure.

Exercise

The number of printing errors per page in a newspaper press was being controlled using a c-chart. The data in Table 5.4 show the number of errors on the sample pages taken from the press every 15 minutes. Calculate the limits and verify if the process is in-control.

(Answer: UCL (c) = 9.3, LCL (c) = 0; process is not-in-control)

SOME NOTES ABOUT ATTRIBUTE CHARTS

1. p-Chart with Varying Sample Size

In the case of p-charts, we may encounter situations in which we may not be able to take the same size sample each time. For example, we may be using a day's production of tool boxes to constitute one sample for controlling defectives due to poor workmanship. The number produced may vary from day to day. Here we need a p-chart that will take samples that vary in size.

The sample size n goes into the calculation of control limits. One way of handling the varying sample size is to use an average value for n if the sample size does not vary too much (not more than 25 percent from the chosen average). This is only an approximate method, but is considered adequate for practical purposes.

A more correct approach would be to calculate individual limits based on the sample size for each sample and to compare the p value from each sample against limits calculated for that sample. The p-chart then looks like what is shown in Figure 5.1. These limits are called stair-step limits because of the way they look.

Part #: I. Tribune										Machine #: 444								Date:				Inspector: KS/C		
Defect type: Ink run smudges										Instruments:								Unit: Page						
Unit #:	1	2	3	4	5	6	7	8	9	10	11	12	13	14	15	16	17	18	19	20	21	22	23	24	25
No. of defects:	7	6	1	2	1	3	7	6	14	2	2	2	1	0	0	1	0	1	2	15	1	3	4	6	3

$$\bar{c} = \Sigma c/K = \ / \ =$$

$$UCL_c = \bar{c} + 3\sqrt{\bar{c}} =$$

$$LCL_c = \bar{c} - 3\sqrt{\bar{c}} =$$

TABLE 5.4 c-CHART

41

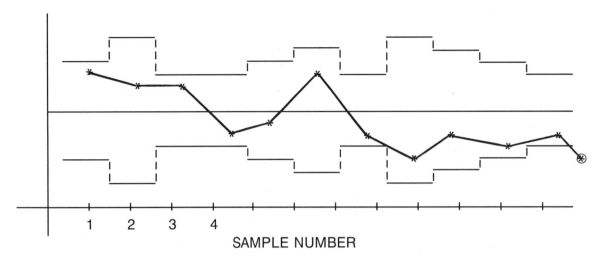

SAMPLE NUMBER

FIGURE 5.1 p-CHART FOR VARYING SAMPLE SIZE WITH STAIR-STEP LIMITS

Using an average n and calculating a constant limit for all samples is easy and convenient from a practical point of view. It can be made more correct if the border line values of p are checked with limits specifically calculated for those samples.

2. np-Chart

If the sample size can be the same when we need a p-chart, we can plot the number of defectives in each sample instead of the fraction defectives computed for each sample.

The best way to calculate the limits for the number of defectives is to first calculate limits for a p-chart and then multiply the limits by the sample size n. The results obtained will be the limits for the number of defectives. This is called the np-chart.

For example, the following two sets of limits would be equivalent in the sense that one or the other could serve the same purpose. With the one on the left, we would plot the p's and with the one on the right we would plot the number of defectives (np's):

p-chart (n = 20)	np-chart
UCL (p) = 0.1	UCL (np) = 2.0
CL (p) = 0.027	CL (np) = 0.54
LCL (p) = 0.0	LCL (np) = 0.0

The advantage in using the np-chart can easily be seen. It allows us to avoid calculating p for each sample while using the chart. However one has to first design a p-chart by calculating p for about 25 samples and then convert the p-chart into an np-chart.

3. Percent Defectives Chart

If instead of multiplying the p-chart limits by n, we multiply them by 100, we will obtain the limits for percent defectives. For example, the following two sets of limits are equivalent:

p-chart	100 p-chart
UCL (p) = 0.1	UCL (100p) = 10.0
CL (p) = 0.027	CL (100p) = 2.7
LCL (p) = 0.0	LCL (100p) = 0.0

With the limits on the left we will plot the fraction defectives (p's), while with the limits on the right we will plot the percent defectives (100p's). The advantage with the percent defectives chart is that we will be working with larger numbers. Also, people usually understand percent defectives better than fraction defectives.

4. Why Do We Need Lower Control Limits on the p-Chart or c-Chart?

The lower control limits do not have the same significance with the p-chart or c-chart as they have with the X-bar chart. Yet we need them because when there is real improvement in the process, the change for the better is signaled by values below the LCL. Of course we have to make sure that such values are not caused by inspector or instrument errors.

5. p-Chart for Many Characteristics

One of the advantages of the p-chart is that one chart can be used for several product characteristics. It is often a good idea to start one p-chart for several characteristics to identify the ones that cause the most problem and then use a p-chart or X-bar chart for those characteristics needing close watch.

6. Use of Runs

The rules that pertain to runs above or below the center line and runs up and down can also be used with the p-chart and the c-chart. These rules are especially useful when the average p is decreasing and there is no lower control limit (LCL = 0). In such circumstances it is only through the runs that we will be able to notice the changes in the average p. Such changes in process average usually lead to review of control limits.

7. Subgrouping

As in X-bar and R charts, proper subgrouping is the key to getting the most out of the p-chart. The subgrouping must be done so as to provide leads to discovering assignable causes when they are present. The following example shows the value of creative subgrouping when processes are controlled and improved using a p-chart. The inspiration for this example came from a case study on the production of stockings by W. Edwards Deming in his book *Quality, Productivity, and Competitive Position*.

Example

This example relates to the assembly of specialty cables which required considerable eye focus, and the final quality depended heavily on operator performance. The assembly line experienced a large number of rejects at final inspection and a quality control consultant was asked to help.

There were 14 assemblers who worked in one shift. The first thing the consultant did was to consider each day's production as a sample and plotted the p-chart with the data from the previous month. Figure 5.2 shows data plotted on the p-chart.

The process was in-control(!) with $\overline{p}$ = 11.5 percent. This was the first time the company managers knew how much was being rejected.

This is an example of an in-control process but with totally unacceptable performance. That the process was in-control only meant the assembly process was producing consistently the same proportion of defectives day after day. In this situation the basis of subgrouping would be changed.

Remember, if a control chart shows an in-control process but the performance is unacceptable, the basis of subgrouping needs to be changed.

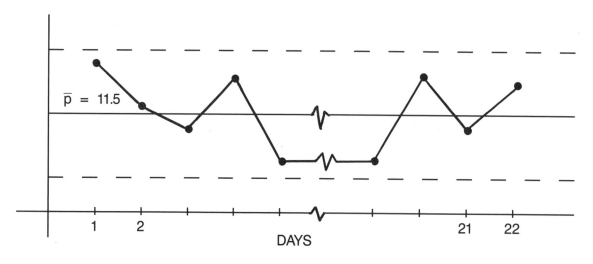

FIGURE 5.2 p-CHART FOR CABLE ASSEMBLY BASED ON DAY'S PRODUCTION

Data were then collected so that each sample represented one week of production by one assembler, and a p-chart was drawn with each sample point representing an assembler. Figure 5.3 shows the p-chart based on the assemblers.

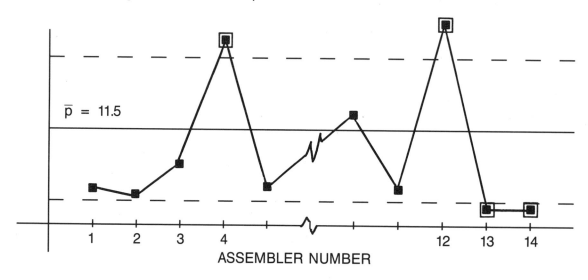

FIGURE 5.3 p-CHART FOR CABLE ASSEMBLY BASED ON ASSEMBLER

The cause of the problem was obvious. Assembler 4 and Assembler 12 were the most important assignable causes. On further investigation, it was found that both assemblers had poor eyesight and needed corrective glasses. The company provided free testing and the glasses. In further pursuance of the assignable cause, the company offered free eye examination for all assemblers and several obtained new prescriptions. Note how an assignable cause is pursued and eradicated so that no further defectives will be produced due to this cause.

The results of these actions were astonishing. The p-chart for the period during which the improvements were made is shown in Figure 5.4. The center line and limits were revised when the process average was becoming markedly lower. The average p for the third month after the investigation started was 0.85 percent.

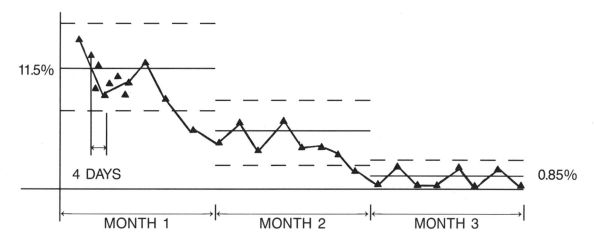

FIGURE 5.4 p-CHART FOR CABLE ASSEMBLY BASED ON DAILY PRODUCTION

The p-chart was then continued based on daily production after finding there were no more differences (statistically speaking) among the assemblers. The daily chart involved less work.

8. u-Chart

The c-chart described previously can be used only if all the units inspected are identical. There are several situations in which an inspection station receives units that are not identical, such as televisions of different sizes, cars of different models, or printed material of different colors and sizes.

If we want to use one chart to cover all different units, we have to use the u-chart which is a modification of the c-chart. It involves defining a standard unit and counting the number of defects per standard unit. Details of the u-chart can be found in the book *Statistical Quality Control* by Grant and Leavenworth.

9. Some Modern Terminology

We have used the traditional names *fraction defective chart* and *defects per unit chart* to describe the p-chart and the c-chart, respectively. In recent times these charts have come to be called the *chart for fraction nonconforming* and the *chart for nonconformities per unit,* respectively.

The term "defective" has traditionally meant that the item does not meet the standards set for it. "Defective" does not necessarily mean that the item is dangerous or unusable. Similarly the term "defect" has been used to mean that the particular feature is undesirable according to the specifications but may or may not render the item rejectable. The terms "nonconforming unit" and "nonconformity" are used to avoid the negative connotation conveyed by the terms "defective" and "defect."

We have used the traditional terms in the belief that as long as we understand the terms they are still usable.

REVIEW

Two basic charts for attribute inspection:
1. The p-chart (fraction defective chart)
2. The c-chart (defects per unit chart)
Limit calculations
These charts are used for continuous improvement of processes.

CHAPTER SIX: SPECIAL CONTROL CHARTS

MOVING AVERAGE AND MOVING RANGE CHARTS

The regular X-bar and R-charts may not be usable in situations where it is not possible to obtain four or five measurements at the same time or in quick succession. Chemical processes are examples of such processes where production cycles are long, and analysis and reporting of sample measurements take time. In these cases, we can use moving average and moving range charts.

These charts also use subgroup averages and ranges, but the method of forming subgroups is different from the regular X-bar and R-charts. Each time there is a new measurement, it is included in the current subgroup. The earliest measurement in the current subgroup is discarded to form a new subgroup. The following example illustrates the method.

Example

The data in Table 6.1 relate to the presence of an impurity in a final product in a chemical plant. The method of computing the moving averages and ranges for n = 3 and the calculation of X-double bar and R-bar, needed for computing limits, are shown in Table 6.1.

The limits for the two charts are calculated using the following formulas:

$$UCL\ (R) = D_4\overline{R} \qquad\qquad UCL\ (\overline{X}) = \overline{\overline{X}} + A_2\overline{R}$$
$$CL\ (R) = \overline{R} \qquad\qquad CL\ (\overline{X}) = \overline{\overline{X}}$$
$$LCL\ (R) = D_3\overline{R} \qquad\qquad LCL\ (\overline{X}) = \overline{\overline{X}} - A_2\overline{R}$$

The factors D_4, D_3, and A_2 are the same as regular X-bar and R-charts.

For the example:

$$UCL\ (R) = D_4\overline{R} = 2.574 \times 1.81 = 4.659$$
$$CL\ (R) = \overline{R} = 1.81$$
$$LCL\ (R) = 0$$
$$UCL\ (\overline{X}) = \overline{\overline{X}} + A_2\overline{R}$$
$$= 6.31 + (1.023)\ (1.81) = 8.162$$
$$CL\ (\overline{X}) = \overline{\overline{X}} = 6.31$$
$$LCL\ (\overline{X}) = \overline{\overline{X}} - A_2\overline{R}$$
$$= 6.31 - (1.023)\ (1.81) = 4.458$$

Averages for batches 60 and 61 are outside the limit. The process is not in-control.

The M-average and M-range charts for the data on percentage impurity are shown drawn on the standard sheet in Table 6.2.

Batch Number	Percent Impurity	Moving Average	Moving Range
54	4.75	——	——
55	5.39	——	——
56	4.98	5.04	0.64
57	6.19	5.52	1.21
58	7.69	6.29	2.71
59	9.02	7.63	2.83
60	9.00	8.57	1.31
61	6.51	8.18	2.51
62	7.10	7.54	2.49
63	5.12	6.24	1.98
64	5.86	6.03	1.98
65	5.18	5.39	0.74
66	5.66	5.57	0.68
67	5.07	5.30	0.59
68	6.18	5.64	1.11
69	7.47	6.24	2.40
70	6.17	6.61	1.30
71	4.99	6.21	2.48
72	6.31	5.82	1.32
73	5.50	5.60	1.32
74	5.52	5.78	0.81
75	5.24	5.42	0.28
76	9.07	6.61	3.83
77	6.15	6.82	3.83
78	5.73	6.98	3.34
		$\Sigma \overline{X}$ = 145.03	ΣR = 41.69

$\overline{\overline{X}}$ = 145.03/23 = 6.31 $\overline{R}$ = 41.69/23 = 1.81

TABLE 6.1 CALCULATION OF MOVING AVERAGE AND MOVING RANGE FOR DATA ON PERCENT IMPURITY IN A CHEMICAL PRODUCT

MOVING AVERAGE AND MOVING RANGE CHARTS

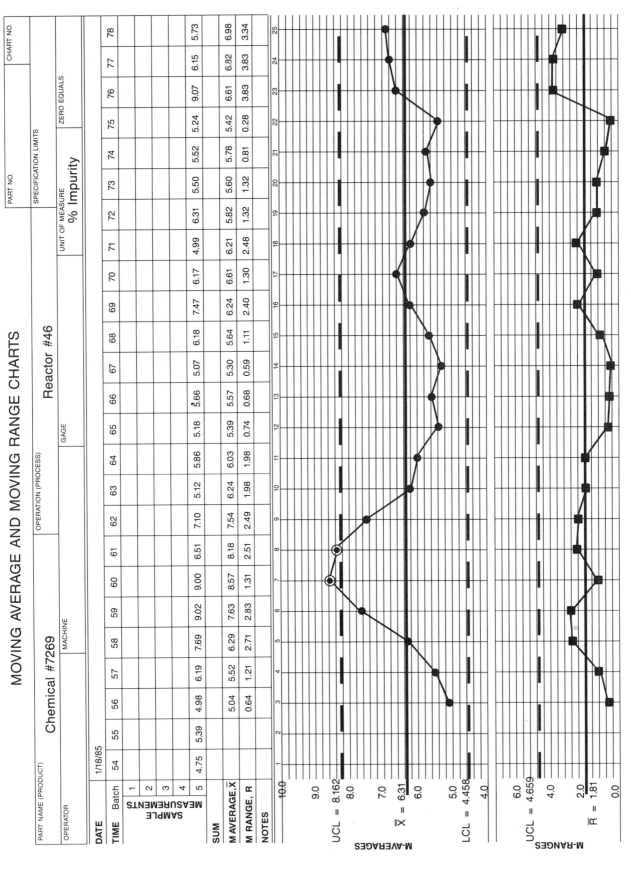

PART NAME (PRODUCT) Chemical #7269   **OPERATION (PROCESS)** Reactor #46   **PART NO.**   **CHART NO.**

OPERATOR   **MACHINE**   **GAGE**   **UNIT OF MEASURE** % Impurity   **SPECIFICATION LIMITS**   **ZERO EQUALS**

DATE 1/18/85

TIME	Batch	54	55	56	57	58	59	60	61	62	63	64	65	66	67	68	69	70	71	72	73	74	75	76	77	78
SAMPLE MEASUREMENTS	1																									
	2																									
	3																									
	4																									
	5	4.75	5.39	4.98	6.19	7.69	9.02	9.00	6.51	7.10	5.12	5.86	5.18	5.66	5.07	6.18	7.47	6.17	4.99	6.31	5.50	5.52	5.24	9.07	6.15	5.73
SUM																										
M AVERAGE, X̄				5.04	5.52	6.29	7.63	8.57	8.18	7.54	6.24	6.03	5.39	5.57	5.30	5.64	6.24	6.61	6.21	5.82	5.60	5.78	5.42	6.61	6.32	6.98
M RANGE, R				0.64	1.21	2.71	2.83	1.31	2.51	2.49	1.98	1.98	0.74	0.68	0.59	1.11	2.40	1.30	2.48	1.32	1.32	0.81	0.28	3.83	3.83	3.34
NOTES																										

M-AVERAGES

UCL = 8.162

$\overline{\overline{X}}$ = 6.31

LCL = 4.458

M-RANGES

UCL = 4.659

$\overline{R}$ = 1.81

TABLE 6.2 VARIABLES CONTROL CHART

If we want to calculate control limits for future use on this process, we could remove the points outside the limits and recalculate the limits with the remaining sample values.

Exercise

Remove those X-bar and R values from the data on percentage impurity given in Table 6.1, and recalculate the limits for moving average and moving range.

(Answer: UCL $(\overline{X})$ = 7.77, LCL $(\overline{X})$ = 4.33, UCL (R) = 4.32, LCL (R) = 0)

NOTES ON MOVING AVERAGE AND MOVING RANGE CHARTS

What Is a Good Value for n?

The moving average and range charts eliminate the noise (variability) in the measurements and disclose the trends in the process. Larger subgroup sizes tend to smooth out the variations and bring out the signals better, but may hide changes that need to be revealed. However, smaller subgroup sizes tend to suffer from excessive fluctuations. Hence subgroup sizes of four or five are recommended.

The subgroup size can also be chosen to reflect what is happening in the process. For example, if three batches of a chemical are produced approximately from one tank car of raw material, a subgroup size of three may make sense.

Caution

We must be careful while reacting to out-of-control points on these charts. Suppose an adjustment is made to a process because of an average value falling outside a limit. The next couple of averages may still be outside the limits because the observations generated when the process was out-of-control may still be in a few subsequent moving subgroups.

Operators must be warned against overreacting to signals from these charts.

Use of Runs on Moving X-Bar and R-Charts

The run rules should be used carefully with the moving average and range charts because the runs do not have the same meaning with these charts as with the regular X-bar and R-charts.

CONTROL CHART FOR INDIVIDUALS (X-CHART)

Again, when four or five observations can not be taken at the same time from a process we can use the chart for individuals. Though the moving average and range charts are preferred in these circumstances, the individual chart has merit because it is simple to use and easy to understand.

The individual chart has to be used along with a chart for successive differences. (This is a moving range chart where subgroup size = 2.) The range chart will disclose excessive variability.

Example

The data shown in Table 6.3 relate to the percent of impurity present in a final product in a chemical plant. Calculation of the successive differences, X-bar and R-bar, are shown in Table 6.3.

Batch Number	Percent Impurity	Successive Difference
54	4.75	——
55	5.39	0.64
56	4.98	0.41
57	6.19	1.21
58	7.69	1.50
59	9.02	1.33
60	9.00	0.02
61	6.51	2.49
62	7.10	0.59
63	5.12	1.98
64	5.86	0.74
65	5.18	0.68
66	5.66	0.48
67	5.07	0.59
68	6.18	1.11
69	7.47	1.29
70	6.17	1.30
71	4.99	1.18
72	6.31	1.32
73	5.50	0.81
74	5.52	0.02
75	5.24	0.28
76	9.07	3.83
77	6.15	2.92
78	5.73	0.42
	$\Sigma X = 155.85$	$\Sigma R = 27.14$

$$\overline{X} = 155.85/25 = 6.23 \qquad \overline{R} = 27.14/24 = 1.13$$

TABLE 6.3 DATA ON PERCENT IMPURITY IN BATCHES OF A CHEMICAL PRODUCED IN A REACTOR

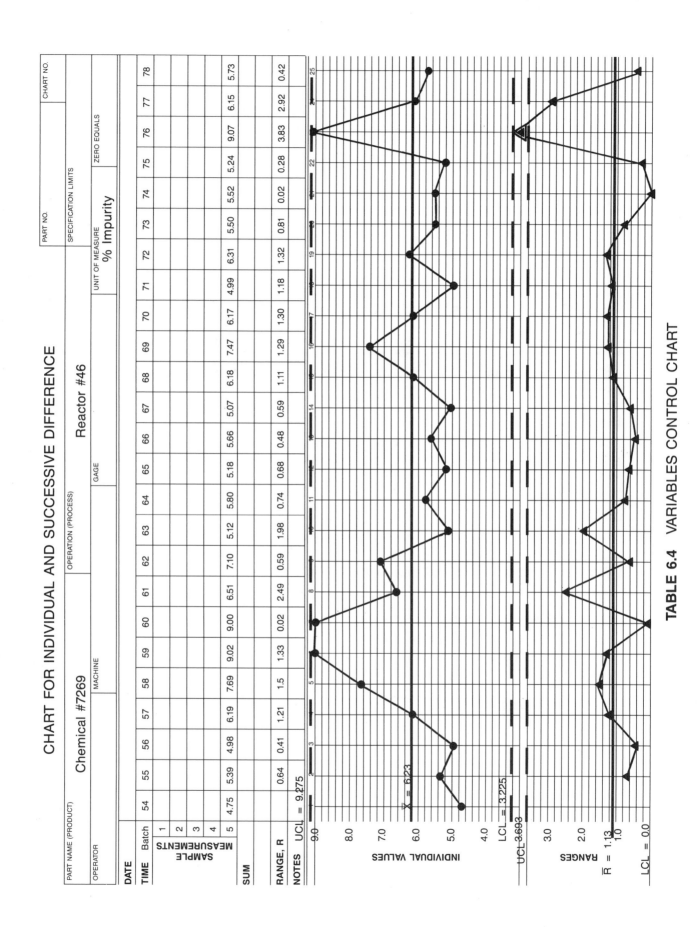

CHART FOR INDIVIDUAL AND SUCCESSIVE DIFFERENCE

PART NAME (PRODUCT): Chemical #7269
OPERATION (PROCESS): Reactor #46
UNIT OF MEASURE: % Impurity

TIME Batch	54	55	56	57	58	59	60	61	62	63	64	65	66	67	68	69	70	71	72	73	74	75	76	77	78
1																									
2																									
3																									
4																									
5	4.75	5.39	4.98	6.19	7.69	9.02	9.00	6.51	7.10	5.12	5.80	5.18	5.66	5.07	6.18	7.47	6.17	4.99	6.31	5.50	5.52	5.24	9.07	6.15	5.73
RANGE, R		0.64	0.41	1.21	1.5	1.33	0.02	2.49	0.59	1.98	0.74	0.68	0.48	0.59	1.11	1.29	1.30	1.18	1.32	0.81	0.02	0.28	3.83	2.92	0.42

NOTES: UCL = 9.275

$\bar{X} = 6.23$
LCL = 3.225
UCL = 3.693
$\bar{R} = 1.13$
LCL = 0.0

INDIVIDUAL VALUES: 9.0, 8.0, 7.0, 6.0, 5.0, 4.0
RANGES: 3.0, 2.0, 1.0

TABLE 6.4 VARIABLES CONTROL CHART

The limits for the two charts are calculated using the following formulas:

$$UCL\ (R) = 3.268\overline{R} \qquad\qquad UCL\ (X) = \overline{X} + 2.659\overline{R}$$

$$CL\ (R) = \overline{R} \qquad\qquad CL\ (X) = \overline{X}$$

$$LCL\ (R) = 0 \qquad\qquad LCL\ (X) = \overline{X} - 2.659\overline{R}$$

For the example:

$$UCL\ (R) = 3.268 \times 1.13 = 3.693$$

$$CL\ (R) = 1.13$$

$$LCL\ (R) = 0$$

$$UCL\ (X) = 6.23 + 2.659 \times 1.13 = 9.235$$

$$CL\ (X) = 6.23$$

$$LCL\ (X) = 6.23 - 2.659 \times 1.13 = 3.225$$

The R value corresponding to batch 76 is outside the limit. The process is not in-control.

The chart for individuals and successive differences for this example is shown in Table 6.4.

It is possible to remove the out-of-control values of X or R and recalculate limits with the remaining values for future control.

Exercise

Calculate the control limits for X and R for controlling the impurity in the future after discarding those values in Table 6.4 that are outside limits.

(Answer: UCL (X) = 8.53, LCL (X) = 3.16; UCL (R) = 3.3, LCL (R) = 0)

REVIEW

When it is not possible to obtain several observations at the same time, we can use either of the following:

- Moving X-bar and moving R-chart
- X-chart and chart for successive differences

Moving X-bar and R-charts are more sensitive and less noisy.

The X-chart is simple and easy to use.

CHAPTER SEVEN: FREQUENCY DISTRIBUTIONS

We have said that there is variability in every population. It is necessary to understand and be able to describe this variability before a population of products can be called good or bad. The frequency distribution enables us to describe the variability in populations.

A frequency distribution simply shows how a population is distributed among various values, within the range of possible values. In order to figure out the distribution of a population, we must take a sample from it and draw the distribution of the sample data. The distribution of the sample data is called the histogram. If the sample is large enough (consisting of 50 or more measurements) the histogram represents the distribution of the population from which the sample is taken.

The method of drawing the histogram from sample data is explained in the following example.

STEPS IN DRAWING THE HISTOGRAM

Step 1

Collect at least 50 observations.

Example

The following numbers represent the weight (in grams) of concentrate in 100 aerosol cans of antiperspirant from an automatic filling line:

20.0	19.5	21.0	20.0	20.5	22.0	22.5	22.5	24.0	23.5
19.0	21.0	21.0	21.0	20.5	20.5	22.5	22.5	23.0	21.5
19.5	20.5	21.0	20.5	21.0	20.0	20.5	23.0	22.0	21.5
20.0	21.5	24.0	23.0	20.0	21.0	22.0	22.0	23.0	22.0
22.5	19.5	21.0	21.5	21.0	22.5	19.5	22.5	22.0	21.0
21.5	20.5	22.0	21.5	23.5	23.0	23.5	21.0	22.0	20.0
19.0	21.5	23.0	21.0	23.5	19.0	20.0	22.0	20.5	22.5
21.0	20.5	19.5	22.0	21.0	21.5	20.5	19.0	19.5	19.5
20.0	23.5	24.0	20.5	21.5	21.0	22.5	20.0	22.0	22.0
22.0	20.5	21.0	22.5	20.0	21.5	23.0	22.0	23.0	18.5

Step 2

Find the smallest and the largest values in the data.

Example

Smallest: 18.5   Largest: 24.0

Step 3

Divide the range into K number of equal cells and determine the cell limits. Use the following table to decide the value for K:

Number of Observations in Data	Value of K
50 or less	6
51 – 100	7
101 – 200	8

These are only approximate rules. The number of cells used can be one more or less than what is given in the table. However, do not use less than five cells.

Example

There are 100 observations in data – use K = 7.

To determine cell limits, the width of each cell is $\frac{(24.0 - 18.5)}{7}$ = 0.786.

Since 0.786 is an inconvenient number, we will use a cell width of 1.0.

This type of adjustment is necessary for the sake of convenience. We will choose cell limits in such a way that:

1. There is no doubt as to where an observation belongs when we try to assign them to cells.

2. The cells should cover the lowest and the highest values in the data.

The cell limits for the example will be as shown in Table 7.1 on the standard sheet. We ended up with six cells, which is acceptable. See Table 7.1 for the remaining steps.

Step 4

Tally the observations into the cells and count the frequencies in each cell. The result is the frequency distribution. Calculate the percent frequency for each cell by dividing each frequency by the number of values in the data, and multiplying by 100. All this can be done on the standard sheet.

Step 5

Draw a graph of the frequency distribution with cells on the horizontal axis and percent frequency on the vertical axis. The resulting graph is the *histogram*.

Step 6

Interpret the histogram. The histogram, if drawn from 50 or more measurements, represents the distribution of the population from which the sample data came. It tells us at approximately which point the values are clustered. In other words, it gives us an idea of the *central tendency* of the population. In the case of weights of concentrate in aerosol cans, the weights are clustered around 21.0.

The histogram also shows how dispersed the values are from the central value. We can also look at the histogram in relation to the specifications. See the following examples of histograms showing how we interpret them in relation to the specifications. In the examples we have approximated the histogram with a smooth curve. The curve is the approximation of the distribution of the population.

Part No.		Part Name Concentrate		Source Line BB			
Characteristic Weight in Grams				Engineering Specification			
Date		Remarks					
Cell Size from - to	Mid-Point	Tally			Freq.	Percent Freq.	Cumul. Percent Freq.
18.1 - 19	18.5	ЖТ			5	5	5
19.1 - 20	19.5	ЖТ ЖТ ЖТ II			17	17	22
20.1 - 21	20.5	ЖТ ЖТ ЖТ ЖТ ЖТ III			28	28	50
21.1 - 22	21.5	ЖТ ЖТ ЖТ ЖТ IIII			24	24	74
22.1 - 23	22.5	ЖТ ЖТ ЖТ III			18	18	92
23.1 - 24	23.5	ЖТ III			8	8	100
				Total	100	100	

TABLE 7.1 FREQUENCY DISTRIBUTION DATA SHEET

Example A

The variability in process is well within the variability allowed by the specifications. The process is centered in relation to the specifications. This is a good situation.

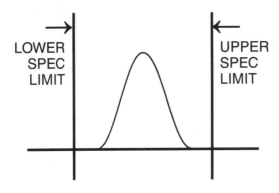

Example B

There is acceptable process variability, but the process needs centering.

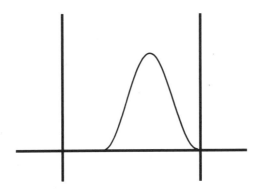

Example C

The process variability is good. Lack of centering already produces out-of-specification products.

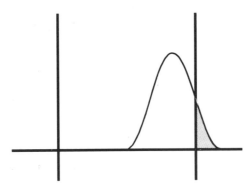

Example D

The process variability is just about equal to that allowed in the specifications. This is not a comfortable situation and needs close control.

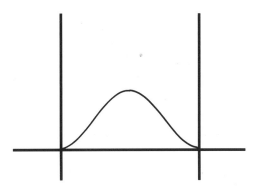

Example E

The process variability equals the variability in the specifications. The process is off center and some scrap will be generated.

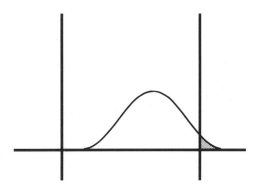

Example F

The process variability is larger than allowed by the specifications. We need to reduce the variability in process.

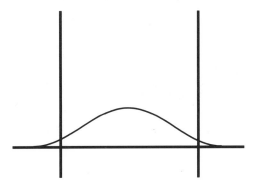

Example G

This is a bi-model distribution. Two different populations are mixed together. Everything is still within specifications.

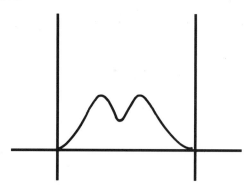

Example H

This is a bi-model distribution. There is a mixture of two processes, and each has acceptable variability. Both need to be centered.

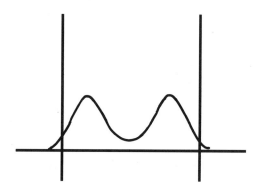

Example I

Everything is within specification, but this may be the result of 100 percent sorting or blending.

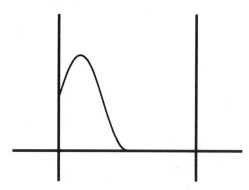

Example J

This shows evidence of sorting except the inspector is passing some out-of-specification material, or the inspector's instrument is not in calibration.

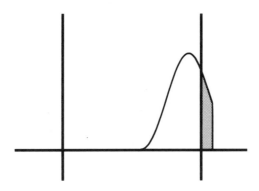

Example K

Apparently the process is good. Perhaps the inspector is making some bad measurements.

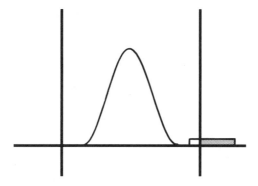

Thus, we can see that the histogram can tell quite a bit about a process. There are many computer programs that generate histograms, given the data. It is necessary to understand how they are drawn to interpret the computer outputs correctly.

Exercise

The following data represent weights of pallet loads of chemical, shipped by a chemical company in pounds above 2,300 pounds. Draw a histogram for the data. If the specification calls for 2,390 ± 10 pounds, how is the packaging operation doing in relation to the specifications?

90	85	96	92	100	87	92	81	86	80
76	72	76	75	50	46	58	58	80	90
81	97	91	89	88	96	96	106	101	98
90	99	108	100	108	89	102	101	85	120
140	150	140	112	90	98	100	102	116	128
101	108	115	111	109	82	88	81	85	85
55	58	68	72	64	69	102	98	91	86
77	81	86	80	85	88	95	89	86	91
80	71	74	72	72	73	72	76	72	68
64	71	96	118	101	86	94	99	91	95
86	91	94	77	85	89	82	115	100	101
100	97	100	98	92	94	97	90	91	88

(Answer: Quite a large proportion outside specification; too large a variability in pallet weights)

REVIEW

We should take into account the variability in a population before saying a population is good or bad.

Frequency distributions enable us to describe this variability.

Frequency distribution of sample data represents the frequency distribution of the population if the sample has been large enough (50 or more).

The method of drawing the frequency distribution of sample data (histogram) was shown.

The histogram tells quite a bit about the population for which it has been drawn.

We can compare histograms with specification limits and make a judgment about the ability of a process to meet a given specification.

CHAPTER EIGHT:
NUMERICAL MEASURES TO DESCRIBE POPULATIONS

We saw in the previous chapter how the histogram drawn from sample data can give a picture of the way the values in a population are distributed. In many situations, we may want to define two other characteristics of a population in terms of numbers: the central tendency and the amount of variability.

The central tendency indicates the value around which the population is distributed. The *average* of all the values in a population is generally used as a measure of central tendency. We will use $\overline{\overline{X}}$ to denote this average.

The variability refers to how far the values are from the average. The magnitude of this variability is usually measured by the quantity: *standard deviation* denoted by the Greek letter σ (sigma).

Thus, for any given population we want to know:

1. The population average: $\overline{\overline{X}}$
2. The population standard deviation: σ
3. The shape of the population distribution:

The exact values of $\overline{\overline{X}}$ or σ, or the exact shape of the distribution of the population are never known, because we cannot measure every item in a population and compute the average or draw the frequency distribution. Therefore, we resort to *estimating* the values of these population parameters from samples.

We already saw how to glean the frequency distribution of a population through the histogram (Figure 8.1). Now we will see how we compute the sample average ($\overline{X}$) and standard deviation (S) as estimates for the population values $\overline{\overline{X}}$ and σ respectively. These measures from sample are called sample statistics.

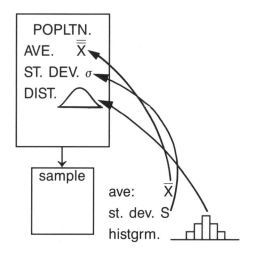

FIGURE 8.1 POPULATION PARAMETERS AND SAMPLE STATISTICS

The $\overline{X}$ and S are computed using the following two formulas:

$$\overline{X} = \frac{\Sigma X}{n}$$

$$S = \sqrt{\frac{\Sigma(X - \overline{X})^2}{n - 1}}$$

Where X is a typical measurement and n is the number of measurements in a sample.

Computing the average is the same as shown in previous chapters. The standard deviation is new. We illustrate the method of computing $\overline{X}$ and S using the following example.

Example

Compute $\overline{X}$ and S for the following sample data, which are the weights of concentrate in 10 cans of shaving cream, in grams.

20.0	19.0	19.5	20.0	22.5
19.5	21.0	20.5	21.5	19.5

$$\overline{X} = \frac{(20.0 + 19.0 + 19.5 + 20.0 + 22.5 + 19.5 + 21.0 + 20.5 + 21.5 + 19.5)}{10}$$

$$= \frac{203}{10}$$

$$= 20.3$$

Calculation of S is shown as follows:

X	$(X - \overline{X})$	$(X - \overline{X})^2$
20.0	-0.3	0.09
19.0	-1.3	1.69
19.5	-0.8	0.64
20.0	-0.3	0.09
22.5	2.2	4.84
19.5	-0.8	0.64
21.0	0.7	0.49
20.5	0.2	0.04
21.5	1.2	1.44
19.5	-0.8	0.64

$$\Sigma(X - \overline{X})^2 = 10.60$$

$$S = \sqrt{\frac{\Sigma(X - \overline{X})^2}{n - 1}} = \sqrt{\frac{10.60}{9}} = 1.085$$

From this method we can see the meaning of S. The quantity S represents how far the individual values are dispersed from their average value. The farther the values are from the average (large variability), the larger the value of S will be. The nearer the values are to the average (small variability), the smaller S will be.

Another formula to calculate S which saves some steps in computation is shown as follows:

$$S = \sqrt{\frac{\Sigma X^2 - (\Sigma X)^2/n}{n - 1}}$$

The standard deviation can be calculated for the weights of shaving cream concentrate using this formula:

X	X²
20.0	400.0
19.0	361.0
19.5	380.25
20.0	400.0
22.5	506.25
19.5	380.25
21.0	441.0
20.5	420.25
21.5	462.25
19.5	380.25
$\Sigma X = 203.0$	$\Sigma X^2 = 4131.5$

$$S = \sqrt{\frac{[4131.5 - (203)^2/10]}{9}} = 1.085$$

Both formulas give the same result. But the second formula is recommended for regular use because it involves less work.

Although modern calculators will perform these calculations with the push of a button, we should know the details of these calculations so we understand the meaning of the results.

COMPUTING $\overline{X}$ AND S FROM LARGE AMOUNTS OF DATA

When we have to calculate these measures from large amounts of data, the formulas given previously involve a considerable amount of work. We can then use the following formulas which involve less work and give approximate results that are good for all practical purposes. In order to use these we first have to group the data into cells as we did for drawing a histogram. These are known as *formulas for grouped data:*

$$\overline{X} = \frac{\Sigma(fX)}{n}$$

$$S = \sqrt{\frac{[\Sigma(fX^2) - (\{\Sigma(fX)\}^2/n)]}{n - 1}}$$

Where X: stands for the midpoint of each cell

f: stands for the number of values in each cell

n: is the total number of values in data

Example

Compute $\overline{X}$ and S for the following grouped data:

Midpoint of cell (X)	Frequency (f)
18.75	5
19.75	17
20.75	28
21.75	24
22.75	17
23.75	9
	Total = 100 = n

$$\Sigma\ (fX)\ =\ (5 \times 18.75) + (17 \times 19.75) + (28 \times 20.75) + (24 \times 21.75) + (17 \times 22.75) + (9 \times 23.75)$$

$$=\ 2133$$

$$\Sigma(fX^2)\ =\ (5 \times 18.75^2) + (17 \times 19.75^2) + (28 \times 20.75^2) + (24 \times 21.75^2) + (17 \times 22.75^2) + (9 \times 23.75^2)$$

$$=\ 45673.25$$

$$\overline{X}\ =\ \frac{\Sigma(fX)}{n}\ =\ \frac{2133}{100}\ =\ 21.33$$

$$S\ =\ \sqrt{\frac{[\Sigma(fX^2) - (\{\Sigma(fX)^2\}/n)]}{n - 1}}$$

$$=\ \sqrt{\frac{[45673.25 - (2133)^2/100)]}{99}}$$

$$=\ \sqrt{1.7814}\ =\ \underline{1.335}$$

USING $\overline{X}$ AND S

If $\overline{X}$ and S have been computed from large enough data (50 or larger values) randomly selected from a population, then they represent the mean ($\overline{\overline{X}}$) and the standard deviation (σ) of the entire population. In many situations involving industrial measurements, these two measures are adequate to draw conclusions about the entire population of products.

We will see in the next chapter how we use these to assess the capability of a process to meet a given specification.

Exercise

Compute $\overline{X}$ and S of the following weights in pounds of chemical packaged in a warehouse.

90	85	96	92	100	87	92	81
86	80	76	72	76	75	50	46
58	58	80	90	81	97	91	89
88	96	96	106	101	98	90	99
108	100	108	89	102	101	85	120
140	150	140	112	90	98	100	102
116	128	101	108	115	111	109	82
88	81	85	85				

(Answer: $\overline{X}$ = 94.3, S = 19.4)

Compute $\overline{X}$ and S for the following grouped data in pounds.

Midpoint	Frequency
55.5	4
75.5	15
95.5	27
111.5	10
135.5	3
155.5	1

(Answer: $\overline{X}$ = 93.5, S = 19.8)

REVIEW

For any population we want to know three things:

   1. Central tendency

   2. Amount of variability

   3. Shape of distribution

These are "measured" respectively by:

   1. Average of Population: $\bar{\bar{X}}$

   2. Standard Deviation of Population: σ

   3. Frequency Distribution of Population:

We can "estimate" the above three using:

   1. Average from a large sample: $\bar{X}$

   2. Standard deviation from a large sample: S

   3. Histogram from a large sample:

CHAPTER NINE:
NORMAL DISTRIBUTION AND PROCESS CAPABILITY

There are several types of distributions of populations as seen in histograms (Figure 9.1). Of all the types, the one we see most often is the bell-shaped curve called the _normal distribution._ Many industrial measurements have this kind of distribution.

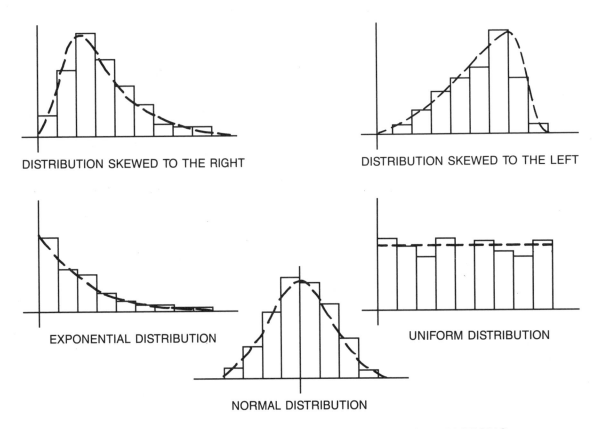

DISTRIBUTION SKEWED TO THE RIGHT

DISTRIBUTION SKEWED TO THE LEFT

EXPONENTIAL DISTRIBUTION

UNIFORM DISTRIBUTION

NORMAL DISTRIBUTION

FIGURE 9.1 A FEW DIFFERENT TYPES OF DISTRIBUTIONS

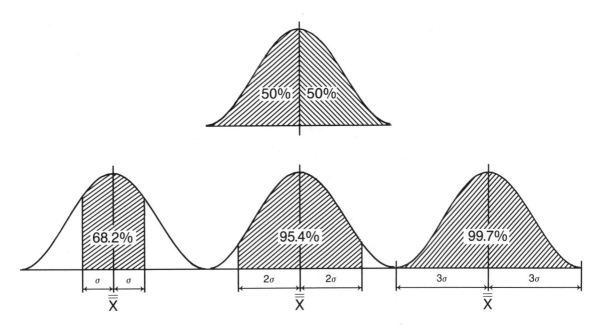

FIGURE 9.2 PROPORTIONS IN DIFFERENT REGIONS
OF A NORMAL DISTRIBUTION

The normal distribution has certain unique characteristics (Figure 9.2):

1. It has the symmetric bell shape with a peak at a value equal to the average of the population.

2. If we use the area enclosed by the curve to represent 100 percent of the population:
   - 50 percent of the population is below, and 50 percent of the population is above the average.
   - 68.2 percent of the population is within 1 standard deviation on either side of the average.
   - 95.4 percent of the population is within 2 standard deviations on either side of the average.
   - 99.7 percent (almost all) of the population will be within 3 standard deviations on either side of the average.

It is interesting to see that proportions of normal populations falling in different regions of values can be determined from the knowledge of the average and standard deviation only. In fact, if the population is normal, the value of the mean together with the value of the standard deviation can tell us about the entire population. This is useful in the study of the process' ability to meet specifications.

ESTIMATING THE MEAN AND STANDARD DEVIATION OF A (NORMAL) POPULATION

We can estimate the mean and standard deviation of a (normal) population in two ways:

1. We can take 50 or more random measurements and compute $\overline{X}$ and S. Then we can use $\overline{X}$ as a population mean ($\overline{\overline{X}}$), and S as the population standard deviation (σ).

2. From control chart data, we can use $\overline{\overline{X}}$ (CL of $\overline{X}$-chart) as the population mean ($\overline{\overline{X}}$) and $\overline{R}/d_2$ (d_2 is a factor available in Table 4.1B) as the population standard deviation (σ).

Once we have the estimates for the mean and standard deviation, we can assess the capability of the process to meet a given set of specifications. We can even calculate, when the process is not fully capable, exactly what percent of the population is within specification and what percent is out of specification. Such a comparison of a process' ability to meet specifications and the corrective action taken to bring the process into specification is called the process capability study.

PROCESS CAPABILITY STUDY

When a process has been brought in-control using control charts, we only know that the process is producing uniformly the _same_ quality. There is no guarantee that the process is producing uniformly _good_ quality. Therefore, the next thing we must do is to check the process against the specifications. If necessary, the process must be adjusted to bring it within specification.

A process that is not-in-control has no definable capability; we should first bring the process in-control before we try to measure its capability.

The process capability study involves knowing the process, knowing the specifications, and comparing the two.

Knowing the Process

We have said that the output from a process can be described by a distribution and that we can make the assumption that most processes are normally distributed. (This can also be verified by a quality engineer.) Further, if a process is normally distributed and if we know its mean and standard deviation, we know about the entire process.

Comparing with the Specifications

When a known process is compared with known specifications, one of the situations shown in Figure 9.3A through 9.3D can arise.

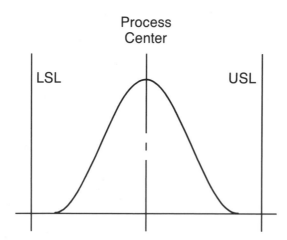

FIGURE 9.3A   THE PROCESS IS CENTERED WITH RESPECT TO SPECIFICATION LIMITS. THE PROCESS VARIABILITY IS WITHIN SPECIFICATION.

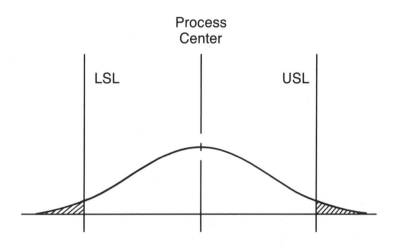

FIGURE 9.3B   THE PROCESS IS CENTERED BUT THE SPREAD IS MORE THAN THE SPECIFICATION WOULD ALLOW

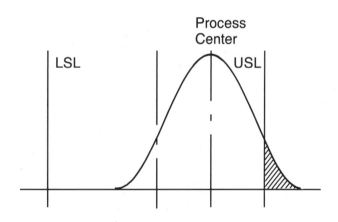

FIGURE 9.3C   THE PROCESS IS OFF CENTER

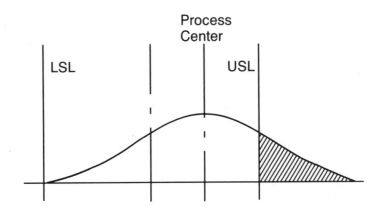

FIGURE 9.3D THE PROCESS HAS TOO LARGE A VARIABILITY AND IS OFF CENTER

Making a histogram from sample data and comparing it with the specifications would show if all the products are within specification or if some of them are outside specification. When all the products are not within specification, adjustment must be made to center the process or reduce the variability. These can be accomplished sometimes by a simple adjustment of a setting, or firmly tightening a fixture. Sometimes it involves extensive experimentation and expensive equipment. The mechanic or the process engineers usually know the best way to adjust the process.

It is important to note that the statistical methods provide a picture of what is happening in the process and point to how it should be improved.

CAPABILITY INDICES

Under certain circumstances we may want to quantify the extent to which a process is capable of meeting a specification. For example, we may want to compare two machines in their ability to meet a given specification, and we may want to quantify each machine's capability for purposes of comparison. In another case, we may want to compare two vendors' ability to supply quality products. Under these circumstances we use the capability indices which enable us to _quantify_ the capability of a process.

The two commonly used capability indices are Cp and Cpk. These are calculated according to the following formulas:

$$\text{Cp} = \frac{\text{spread in specification}}{\text{spread in process}}$$

$$= \frac{\text{USL} - \text{LSL}}{6\sigma}$$

where USL and LSL are specification limits and σ is the estimated process standard deviation.

The Cp index simply compares the natural variability in the process, which is given by 6σ, with the variability allowed in specification. If the value of Cp is less than 1.0, the process is producing scrap. It is usually stipulated that the value of Cp should be larger than 1.33 to guarantee that the variability of the processes is well within allowable variability. Then any small changes in process average will not cause scrap. The larger the value of Cp the better the process (Figure 9.4).

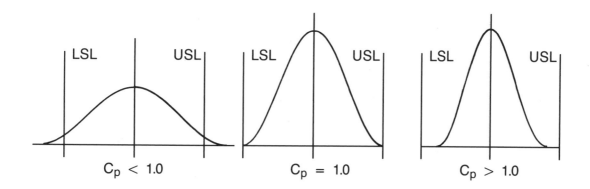

FIGURE 9.4   PROCESSES WITH DIFFERENT C_p VALUES

The Cp index works very well as long as the process is centered in regard to the specification. There may be a situation where the process has a good Cp value, yet scrap is produced because the process is off-center. In other words the Cp index *does not* measure the centering of the process. This drawback is avoided in the next capability index, Cpk.

$$Cpk = \frac{\text{distance between process center and the nearest specification}}{3\sigma}$$

$$= \frac{\text{smaller of } [(USL - \overline{\overline{X}}), (\overline{\overline{X}} - LSL)]}{3\sigma}$$

If the value of Cpk is less than 1.0, the process is producing scrap. Again, a value of Cpk larger than 1.33 would guarantee that the process will remain comfortably within specification. Figure 9.5 illustrates the meaning of this index.

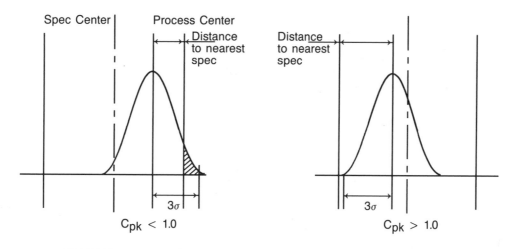

FIGURE 9.5   PROCESSES WITH DIFFERENT C_{pk} VALUES

Example

A process that has been brought to control had process average $\overline{\overline{X}}$ = 41.5 and $\overline{R}/d_2$ = 0.92. If the specification for the process calls for values between 39 and 47, calculate the capability indices Cp and Cpk for this process in its present condition.

$$Cp = \frac{(47 - 39)}{(6 \times 0.92)} = 1.45$$

$$Cpk = \frac{\text{smaller of } \{(47 - 41.5), (41.5 - 39)\}}{(3 \times .92)}$$

$$= \frac{\text{smaller of } (5.5, 2.5)}{(3 \times 0.92)}$$

$$= \frac{2.5}{(3 \times 0.92)}$$

$$= 0.906$$

The process passed the Cp test because of small variability, but failed the Cpk test due to lack of centering (Figure 9.6).

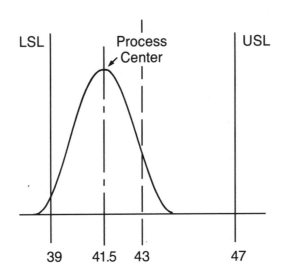

FIGURE 9.6   A PROCESS WITH GOOD C_p BUT POOR C_{pk}

The Cpk is a superior index for measuring the capability of processes because it checks on process centering as well as process variability. It can be used:

1. To track capability of processes over time.
2. To prioritize processes for attention for improvement projects.
3. To certify suppliers' processes, etc.

Exercise

$\overline{X}$ and R control charts were maintained on the width of labels cut on an automatic press, with subgroup size = 4. After the process was brought in-control, the $\overline{\overline{X}}$ = 2.10 and $\overline{R}$ = 0.06. If the customer's specification calls for a tolerance of 2.125 $\pm$ 0.125, what is the Cp Index for this process? What is the Cpk Index for the process? What is your recommendation?

(Answer: Cp = 1.44, Cpk = 1.15, Cpk can be improved by centering)

USE OF NORMAL TABLES

In certain situations we may have to predict exactly how much of the total product will be below the specification limit, outside of specification, or above a certain value. We may come across specifications such as, "not more than 1.5 percent of the boxes should have less than 15 oz." We need to know how to use the normal tables in order to interpret and follow these specifications.

A population that has normal distribution with average = 0 and standard deviation = 1.0 is said to have the *standard normal distribution*. Table 9.1 gives the areas under this standard normal curve outside of any value Z, and is called the standard normal tables or simply the normal table. The normal table comes in different versions. The one shown in Table 9.1 is good for quality control work.

The method of using this table to predict proportions of any normally distributed population in any region is shown in Example A. Example B shows how, using the normal distribution model, we can know exactly what we have in a process and know what to do with it.

Example A

The net weight of a chemical in 50-pound bags filled on a filling line, which is in-control, is known to have normal distribution with average = 49.5 pounds and standard deviation = 0.4 pounds.

- If any bag having a net weight of less than 49 pounds is underweight, what proportion of these bags are underweight?

- If the packager does not want to fill any bag with more than 51 pounds, what proportion of the bags have overfill?

Step 1

Calculate the Z score for the lower and upper specifications.

$$\text{Z-lower} = \frac{(\text{average} - \text{LSL})}{\text{standard deviation}}$$

$$\text{Z-upper} = \frac{(\text{USL} - \text{average})}{\text{standard deviation}}$$

The Z score tells us the number of standard deviations a given specification is from the average of the process.

For the first part of the example:

$$\text{Z-lower} = \frac{(49.5 - 49)}{0.4} = 1.25$$

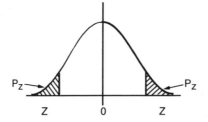

Area Under Standard Normal Curve Outside Z

Z	0.00	0.01	0.02	0.03	0.04	0.05	0.06	0.07	0.08	0.09
3.5	.00023	.00022	.00022	.00021	.00020	.00019	.00019	.00018	.00017	.00017
3.4	.00034	.00033	.00031	.00030	.00029	.00028	.00027	.00026	.00025	.00024
3.3	.00048	.00047	.00045	.00043	.00042	.00040	.00039	.00038	.00036	.00035
3.2	.00069	.00066	.00064	.00062	.00060	.00058	.00056	.00054	.00052	.00050
3.1	.00097	.00094	.00090	.00087	.00085	.00082	.00079	.00076	.00074	.00071
3.0	.00135	.00131	.00126	.00122	.00118	.00114	.00111	.00107	.00104	.00100
2.9	.0019	.0018	.0017	.0017	.0016	.0016	.0015	.0015	.0014	.0014
2.8	.0026	.0025	.0024	.0023	.0023	.0022	.0021	.0021	.0020	.0019
2.7	.0035	.0034	.0033	.0032	.0031	.0030	.0029	.0028	.0027	.0026
2.6	.0047	.0045	.0044	.0043	.0041	.0040	.0039	.0038	.0037	.0036
2.5	.0062	.0060	.0059	.0057	.0055	.0054	.0052	.0051	.0049	.0048
2.4	.0082	.0080	.0078	.0075	.0073	.0071	.0069	.0068	.0066	.0064
2.3	.0107	.0104	.0102	.0099	.0096	.0094	.0091	.0089	.0087	.0084
2.2	.0139	.0136	.0132	.0129	.0125	.0122	.0119	.0116	.0113	.0110
2.1	.0179	.0174	.0170	.0166	.0162	.0158	.0154	.0150	.0146	.0143
2.0	.0228	.0222	.0217	.0212	.0207	.0202	.0197	.0192	.0188	.0183
1.9	.0287	.0281	.0274	.0268	.0262	.0256	.0250	.0244	.0239	.0233
1.8	.0359	.0351	.0344	.0336	.0329	.0322	.0314	.0307	.0301	.0294
1.7	.0446	.0436	.0427	.0418	.0409	.0401	.0392	.0384	.0375	.0367
1.6	.0548	.0537	.0526	.0516	.0505	.0495	.0485	.0475	.0465	.0455
1.5	.0668	.0655	.0643	.0630	.0618	.0606	.0594	.0582	.0571	.0559
1.4	.0808	.0793	.0778	.0764	.0749	.0735	.0721	.0708	.0694	.0681
1.3	.0968	.0951	.0934	.0918	.0901	.0885	.0869	.0853	.0838	.0823
1.2	.1151	.1131	.1112	.1093	.1075	.1057	.1038	.1020	.1003	.0985
1.1	.1357	.1335	.1314	.1292	.1271	.1251	.1230	.1210	.1190	.1170
1.0	.1587	.1562	.1539	.1515	.1492	.1469	.1446	.1423	.1401	.1379
0.9	.1841	.1814	.1788	.1762	.1736	.1711	.1685	.1660	.1635	.1611
0.8	.2119	.2090	.2061	.2033	.2005	.1977	.1949	.1922	.1894	.1867
0.7	.2420	.2389	.2358	.2327	.2297	.2266	.2236	.2207	.2177	.2148
0.6	.2743	.2709	.2676	.2643	.2611	.2578	.2546	.2514	.2483	.2451
0.5	.3085	.3050	.3015	.2981	.2946	.2912	.2877	.2843	.2810	.2776
0.4	.3446	.3409	.3372	.3336	.3300	.3264	.3228	.3192	.3156	.3121
0.3	.3821	.3783	.3745	.3707	.3669	.3632	.3594	.3557	.3520	.3483
0.2	.4207	.4168	.4129	.4090	.4052	.4013	.3974	.3936	.3897	.3859
0.1	.4602	.4562	.4522	.4483	.4443	.4404	.4364	.4325	.4286	.4247
0.0	.5000	.4960	.4920	.4880	.4840	.4801	.4761	.4721	.4681	.4641

TABLE 9.1 NORMAL TABLES

For the second part of the example:

$$\text{Z-upper} = \frac{(51 - 49.5)}{0.4} = 3.75$$

Step 2

Look in the normal table for the proportion outside of the Z scores. This is denoted by Pz in the table.

For the first part of the example:

$$Pz = 0.1057 \text{ (10.57 percent)}$$

For the second part of the example:

$$Pz = 0.00 \text{ (0.0 percent)}$$

(For practical purposes take Pz = 0 for Z > 3.5)
Total outside specification = 10.57 percent (Figure 9.7).

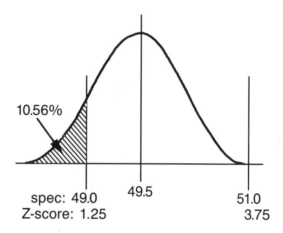

10.56%

spec: 49.0   49.5   51.0
Z-score: 1.25   3.75

FIGURE 9.7   50-LB BAGS OUTSIDE SPECIFICATIONS

Example B

A filling machine that fills 16-oz bottles of soda is in-control. It fills an average of 16 oz and has a standard deviation of 0.2 oz. Government regulations specify that no more than 2.5 percent of the bottles should have less than 15 oz of soda in them.

Determine the percentage of bottles currently below the government specification. Also determine the lowest average the filler can be adjusted to so that the specification can still be satisfied.

For the first part of the example:

$$\text{Z-lower} = \frac{(16 - 15)}{0.2} = 5.0$$

Proportion outside: Pz = 0.000

Currently there is no underfill.

For the second part of the example:

Find the Z score from the table outside of which lies 0.0250 of the population. In other words, find Z for which Pz = 0.0250.

From the Table, Z = 1.96 for Pz = 0.0250. The average can be located 1.96 sigma distance from the specification, and there will be no more than 2.5 percent rejects. So, the target can be (Figure 9.8):

$$15 + 1.96 \times 0.2 = 15.392, \text{ say } 15.4 \text{ gm}$$

Note the savings realized from targeting the process at a lower level. This is possible because the process has a smaller variability than the government has allowed.

This drives home the point that the smaller the variability in a process, the more attainable are the economics.

These examples have shown how the normal distribution model enables us to understand what is happening in a process, predict what will happen to the process, and where possible, enable us to control the process where we want it to be.

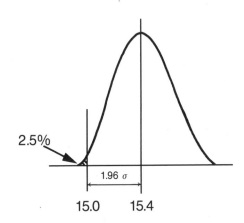

FIGURE 9.8 TARGETING SODA FILLER

Exercise

The amount of perfume shot into cans of deodorant spray is in-control as shown by X-bar and R-charts, with $\overline{\overline{X}}$ = 0.145 grams and $\overline{R}$ = 0.008, subgroup size = 5. The specification calls for 0.1446 ± 0.0043 grams. Find out the percentage of cans receiving less than specification and those receiving more than specification (d_2 = 2.326).

(Answer: Less than specification = 8.38 percent
          More than specification = 12.51 percent)

If no can should have less than 0.14 grams of perfume, what should be the target amount of perfume to be shot into the cans? For practical purposes, assume that for a normally distributed characteristic the proportion outside of 3.5 σ distance from the center is zero.

(Answer: 0.152 gm)

REVIEW

Normal distribution is the most common type of distribution in industrial statistics.

Normally distributed populations have certain unique characteristics.

The average value $\bar{\bar{X}}$ and standard deviation σ of normal populations can tell us all about the population.

$\bar{\bar{X}}$ and σ can be estimated from two methods.

1. From 50 or more measurements:
   - Process average $= \bar{X}$
   - Process standard deviation $= S$
2. From control chart data:
   - Process average $= \bar{\bar{X}}$
   - Process standard deviation $= \bar{R}/d_2$

Process capability analysis involves comparing what we have in our process with what is required by the specifications.

Two capability indices, Cp and Cpk, are used to measure process capability.

CHAPTER TEN: SAMPLING PLANS

Sampling plans generally are used by the customer to verify the product's conformity to specifications after the product has been produced. Sampling plans are used where it is uneconomical or impossible to do 100 percent inspection.

There are two major categories of sampling plans:

1. Sampling Plans for Attribute Inspection
2. Sampling Plans for Measurement (or Variable) Inspection

The sampling plans for attribute inspection that require classification of product as acceptable and rejectable, are easy to follow and use. However, sampling plans for variables are rather complicated.

Under each category there are single sampling plans, double sampling plans, multiple sampling plans, etc. The single sampling plans are simple and easy to learn and use; the double and multiple sampling plans, although more complicated, require less inspection.

We will restrict our discussions here to only the single sampling plans for attributes. Most sampling needs can be met using single sampling plans and these are also the most commonly used plans in industry.

SINGLE SAMPLING PLANS

A single sampling plan is defined by two numbers — n and c; n is called the sample size and c is called the acceptance number.

Suppose we use a single sampling plan with n = 12 and c = 1. This means that we have to take a sample of 12 items from a lot submitted for inspection and if no more than 1 defective is found in the sample we accept the lot, otherwise we reject it.

In this case a lot may be a skidful of cans, a boxful of valves, or one day's production of flow meters. The plan tells us to accept or reject the lot based on what we see in the sample.

SELECTING A SINGLE SAMPLING PLAN

When we are faced with choosing a sampling plan we have numerous alternatives to choose from, such as (10,0), (12,0), (13,1), (24,2), etc. Which is a good sampling plan? How do we choose the one for our needs?

Every sampling plan has an operating characteristic curve (OC curve). The OC curve tells us how the plan will accept or reject lots of different quality. The graph in Figure 10.1 is an example of an OC curve. The sampling plan corresponding to this OC curve would accept lots with 1 percent defectives with 90 percent probability and lots with 8 percent defectives with 10 percent probability.

The OC curve is used as the yardstick to measure how strict or lenient a sampling plan will be.

For any given sampling plan the OC curve can be drawn by computing the probabilities of acceptance by the plan of lots of different quality, the quality of a lot being denoted by the fraction defectives present in it.

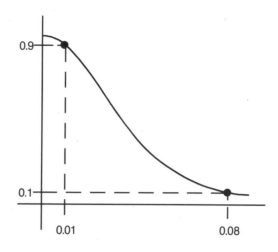

FIGURE 10.1 EXAMPLE OF AN OC CURVE

For a practical understanding, probability can be interpreted as follows: If a lot has probability of 0.9 of acceptance by a sampling plan, it could mean that if 100 such lots are submitted for inspection by the sampling plan, about 90 will be accepted while about 10 will be rejected. Properly chosen sampling plans will have high probability (such as .95 or .99) of passing good lots and will have low probability (such as .10 and .05) of accepting bad lots.

The method of calculating probability of acceptance by a sampling plan is shown in the following example.

Example

A lot made up of 200 items has 12 percent defectives. What is the probability that this lot will be accepted by a single sampling plan with n = 20 and c = 2?

We have to find the probability that a sample of 20 taken from the lot will have no more than two defectives. The theoretically correct probability can be computed using binomial distribution.

A shortcut method involves the use of Table 10.1, known as the Poisson Tables. This method is good as long as n is large (larger than 15).

The method consists of the following steps:

Step 1

Calculate (np), where p is the fraction defectives in the lot.

Step 2

Choose the column on the table that corresponds to the value of (np).

Step 3

Choose the row corresponding to the value of c.

c/np	.01	.05	.10	.20	.30	.40	.50	.60	.70	.80	.90	1.00
0	.990	.951	.904	.818	.740	.670	.606	.548	.496	.449	.406	.367
1	.999	.998	.995	.982	.963	.938	.909	.878	.844	.808	.772	.735
2		.999	.999	.998	.996	.992	.985	.976	.965	.952	.937	.919
3				.999	.999	.999	.998	.996	.994	.990	.986	.981
4							.999	.999	.999	.998	.997	.996
5										.999	.999	.999

c/np	1.10	1.20	1.30	1.40	1.50	1.60	1.70	1.80	1.90	2.00	2.10	2.20
0	.332	.301	.272	.246	.223	.201	.182	.165	.149	.135	.122	.110
1	.699	.662	.626	.591	.557	.524	.493	.462	.433	.406	.379	.354
2	.900	.879	.857	.833	.808	.783	.757	.730	.703	.676	.649	.622
3	.974	.966	.956	.946	.934	.921	.906	.891	.874	.857	.838	.819
4	.994	.992	.989	.985	.981	.976	.970	.963	.955	.947	.937	.927
5	.999	.998	.997	.996	.995	.993	.992	.989	.986	.983	.979	.975
6		.999	.999	.999	.999	.998	.998	.997	.996	.995	.994	.992
7							.999	.999	.999	.998	.998	.998
8										.999	.999	.999

c/np	2.30	2.40	2.50	2.60	2.70	2.80	2.90	3.00	3.50	4.00	4.50	5.00
0	.100	.090	.082	.074	.067	.060	.055	.049	.030	.018	.011	.006
1	.330	.308	.287	.267	.248	.231	.214	.199	.135	.091	.061	.040
2	.596	.569	.543	.518	.493	.469	.445	.423	.320	.238	.173	.124
3	.799	.778	.757	.736	.714	.691	.669	.647	.536	.433	.342	.265
4	.916	.904	.891	.877	.862	.847	.831	.815	.725	.628	.532	.440
5	.970	.964	.957	.950	.943	.934	.925	.916	.857	.785	.702	.615
6	.990	.988	.985	.982	.979	.975	.971	.966	.934	.889	.831	.762
7	.997	.996	.995	.994	.993	.991	.990	.988	.973	.948	.913	.866
8	.999	.999	.998	.998	.998	.997	.996	.996	.990	.978	.959	.931
9			.999	.999	.999	.999	.999	.998	.996	.991	.982	.968
10								.999	.998	.997	.993	.986
11										.999	.997	.994
12											.999	.997
13												.999

c/np	5.50	6.00	6.50	7.00	7.50	8.00	8.50	9.00	9.50	10.0	15.0	20.0
0	.004	.002	.001	.000	.000	.000	.000	.000	.000	.000	.000	.000
1	.026	.017	.011	.007	.004	.003	.001	.001	.000	.000	.000	.000
2	.088	.061	.043	.029	.020	.013	.009	.006	.004	.002	.000	.000
3	.201	.151	.111	.081	.059	.042	.030	.021	.014	.010	.000	.000
4	.357	.285	.223	.172	.132	.099	.074	.054	.040	.029	.002	.000
5	.528	.445	.369	.300	.241	.191	.149	.115	.088	.067	.007	.000
6	.686	.606	.526	.449	.378	.313	.256	.206	.164	.130	.018	.000
7	.809	.743	.672	.598	.524	.452	.385	.323	.268	.220	.037	.002
8	.894	.847	.791	.729	.661	.592	.523	.455	.391	.332	.069	.005
9	.946	.916	.877	.830	.776	.716	.652	.587	.521	.457	.118	.010
10	.974	.957	.933	.901	.862	.815	.763	.705	.645	.583	.184	.021
11	.989	.979	.966	.946	.920	.888	.848	.803	.751	.696	.267	.039
12	.995	.991	.983	.973	.957	.936	.909	.875	.836	.791	.363	.066
13	.998	.996	.992	.987	.978	.965	.948	.926	.898	.864	.465	.104
14	.999	.998	.997	.994	.989	.982	.972	.958	.940	.916	.568	.156
15		.999	.998	.997	.995	.991	.986	.977	.966	.951	.664	.221
16			.999	.999	.998	.996	.993	.988	.982	.974	.748	.297
17					.999	.998	.997	.994	.991	.985	.819	.381
18						.999	.998	.997	.995	.992	.875	.470
19							.999	.998	.998	.996	.917	.559
20								.999	.999	.998	.946	.643
21										.999	.967	.720
22											.980	.787
23											.988	.843
24											.993	.887
25											.996	.922
26											.998	.947
27											.999	.965
28												.978
29												.986
30												.991
31												.995
32												.997
33												.998
34												

TABLE 10.1 CUMULATIVE POISSON PROBABILITIES

Step 4

Read the probability of c or less defectives, which is the probability of acceptance by the plan.

Example

$$np = (20)(0.12) = 2.4$$

$$c = 2$$

Probability of acceptance (Pa) = Probability (2 or less defectives) = 0.569

Incidentally, this example has an important message. We took 10 percent of the lot in the sample and would accept the lot if no more than 10 percent of the sample was defective.

The example shows that if we use such a 10 percent rule we will be accepting lots with 12 percent defectives (very bad lots) about six out of 10 times. This is not a good situation.

There are many people in industry who use 10 percent rules for lack of better information. They should be alerted to the perils of using such rules. Also note that the OC curve calculations enable us to know what we are getting into when we use sampling inspection.

DRAWING THE OC CURVE

Using the previous method we can draw the OC curve of any single sampling plan.

Example

Draw the OC curves for the following single sampling plans:

(20,1), (20,2), (30,1)

In order to draw the OC curves we should choose some convenient values for lot quality (p's), find the corresponding probabilities of acceptance (Pa's) and draw the curves as shown in Figure 10.2.

We see from Figure 10.2 that when we increase the sample size or decrease the acceptance number, the OC curve becomes more and more discriminating between good and bad lots.

Exercise

Draw the OC curves of single sampling plans: (10,0), (10,1), (15,1)

SAMPLING PLAN FOR A GIVEN OC CURVE

The previous discussion relates to drawing the OC curve for a given sampling plan. However, a quality control professional often has to choose a single sampling plan for a given OC curve. First we need to know how to specify a desired OC curve.

Figure 10.3 shows an OC curve that is known as the ideal OC curve. The sampling plan that has this OC curve would discriminate between good and bad lots perfectly. Any lot having quality better than acceptable quality (0.005) will be accepted with probability 1.0; those lots with quality worse than the acceptable quality will be rejected with probability 1.0.

Such a sampling plan would require sample sizes of infinity! We may have to settle for less ideal and more practical sampling plans. We can designate the OC curve we want by specifying one or two points on it.

P	0.01	0.03	0.05	0.07	0.09	0.11	0.13	0.15	0.20
Pa(20,1)	0.982	0.878	0.735	0.591	0.462	0.354	0.267	0.199	0.091
Pa(20,2)	0.998	0.976	0.919	0.833	0.730	0.622	0.518	0.423	0.238
Pa(30,1)	0.963	0.772	0.557	0.379	0.248	0.156	0.095	0.061	0.017

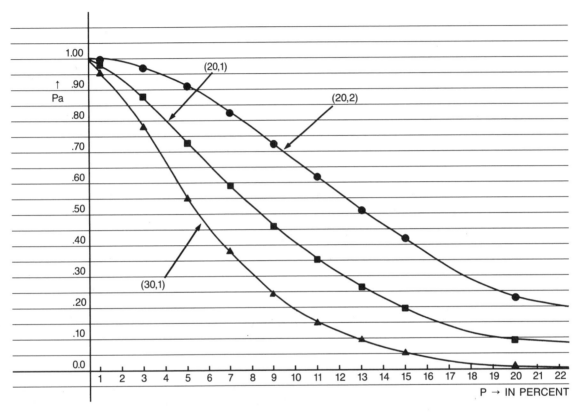

FIGURE 10.2 OC CURVES OF SINGLE SAMPLING PLANS

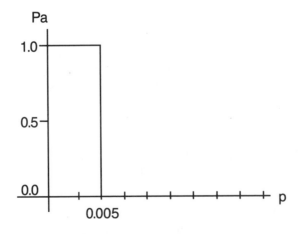

FIGURE 10.3 IDEAL OC CURVE

TERMS

Acceptable quality level (AQL). The maximum percent defective that is still considered good.

Lot tolerance percent defective (LTPD). The worst percent defective that can be tolerated.

Alpha (α). Producer's risk. The probability of rejecting lots of AQL quality.

Beta (β). Consumer's risk. The probability of accepting lots of LTPD quality.

Figure 10.4 shows the relationship of these quantities to each other and the fact that these refer to points on an OC curve.

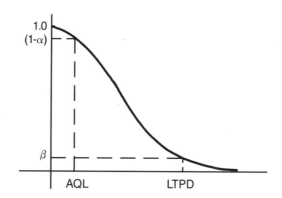

FIGURE 10.4   SPECIFYING AN OC CURVE

The vendor and buyer agree on the values of AQL, α or LTPD, β, or both at the time of writing the contract. Then a sampling plan is chosen that will have an OC curve passing through these points.

The availability of standard tables such as MIL-STD-105D makes it easy to choose sampling plans. MIL-STD-105D gives plans based on AQL, α values. In other words, the plans chosen from MIL-STD-105D will have OC curves passing through the designated AQL, α point.

Similarly there are sampling plans known as Dodge-Romig plans that will have OC curves passing through a given LTPD, β point. Since MIL-STD-105D is the the more popular source for sampling plans in industry, we will restrict our discussion to these plans only.

MIL-STD-105D

This standard provides single sampling plans, double sampling plans, and multiple sampling plans for several AQL values. All plans have the probability of acceptance between 0.95 and 0.99 at the designated AQL. Here we will discuss only single sampling plans.

MIL-STD-105D provides for three levels of inspection: normal, reduced, and tightened. Switching rules (Figure 10.5 shows the essentials of switching rules) provides for how the levels are to be changed depending on vendor performance.

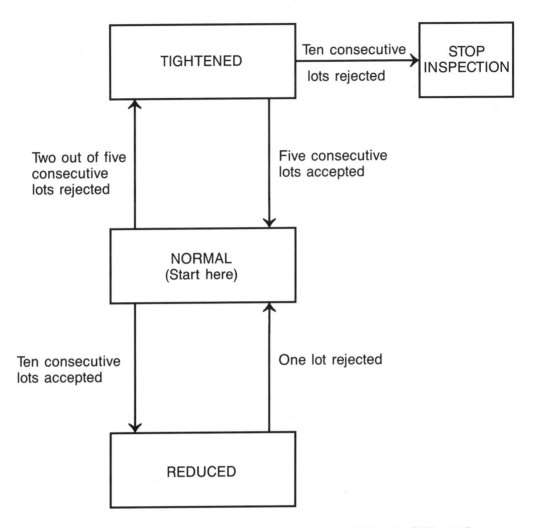

FIGURE 10.5 ESSENTIALS OF SWITCHING RULES FOR MIL-STD-105D
(For more information see MIL-STD-105D, available from the Superintendent of Documents,
U.S. Government Printing Office Washington, DC 20402, document number 343-514/A3330.)

Selection of a sampling plan from this standard is based on lot size. If we know the size of the lot and the AQL we want, we can choose a sampling plan.

Step 1

Enter the table (Table 10.2) that specifies the sample size code based on lot size. Use general inspection level II and the normal inspection table for ordinary use.

Example

Lot size: 200

Desired AQL: 2.5 percent

Code letter (from table) = G

Step 2

Choose the appropriate table. The tables are titled according to level of inspection (normal/reduced/tightened) and according to number of samples in the plan (single/double/multiple). The single sampling tables have been reproduced as Tables 10.3 to 10.5.

LOT OR BATCH SIZE	SPECIAL INSPECTION LEVELS				GENERAL INSPECTION LEVELS		
	S-1	S-2	S-3	S-4	I	II	III
2 to 8	A	A	A	A	A	A	B
9 to 15	A	A	A	A	A	B	C
16 to 25	A	A	B	B	B	C	D
26 to 50	A	B	B	C	C	D	E
51 to 90	B	B	C	C	C	E	F
91 to 150	B	B	C	D	D	F	G
151 to 280	B	C	D	E	E	G	H
281 to 500	B	C	D	E	F	H	J
501 to 1200	C	C	E	F	G	J	K
1201 to 3200	C	D	E	G	H	K	L
3201 to 10000	C	D	F	G	J	L	M
10001 to 35000	C	D	F	H	K	M	N
35001 to 150000	D	E	G	J	L	N	P
150001 to 500000	D	E	G	J	M	P	Q
500001 and over	D	E	H	K	N	Q	R

TABLE 10.2 SAMPLE SIZE CODE LETTERS (MIL-STD-105D)

Example

Single sampling plans for normal inspection: (32,2,3), indicate sample size, acceptance number, and rejection number, respectively.

Similarly we can determine the single sampling plans for tightened inspection (32,1,2) and for reduced inspection (13,1,3).

Note

For single sampling plans, the rejection number is usually 1 + acceptance number, except for reduced inspection. For reduced inspection, if the number of defectives is between the acceptance number and the rejection number, accept the lot but revert to normal inspection.

The OC curves for the plans are also provided in the standard. This helps us understand how the chosen plan will perform against different quality lots. An example of the table giving the OC curves is shown in Table 10.6.

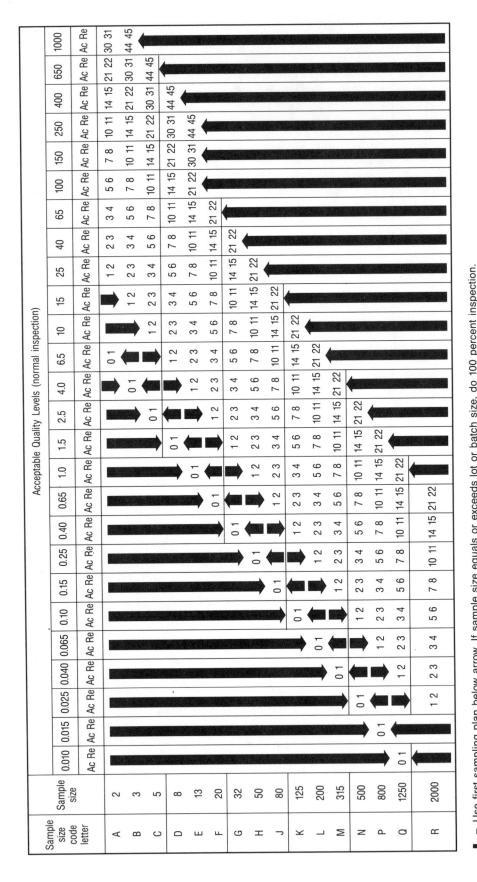

■→ = Use first sampling plan below arrow. If sample size equals or exceeds lot or batch size, do 100 percent inspection.
←■ = Use first sampling plan above arrow.
Ac = Acceptance number.
Re = Rejection number.

TABLE 10.3   SINGLE SAMPLING PLANS FOR NORMAL INSPECTION (MASTER TABLE) (MIL-STD-105D)

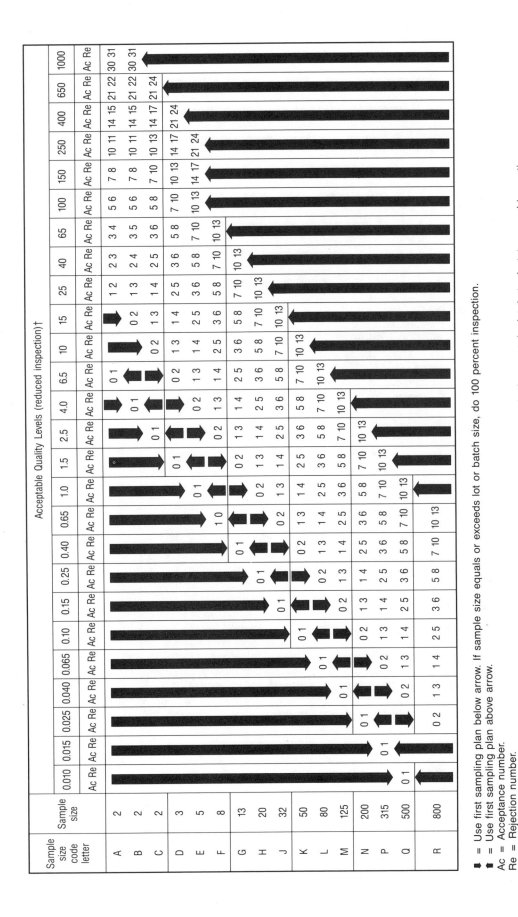

TABLE 10.4   SINGLE SAMPLING PLANS FOR REDUCED INSPECTION (MASTER TABLE) (MIL-STD-105D)

➡ = Use first sampling plan below arrow. If sample size equals or exceeds lot or batch size, do 100 percent inspection.

⬅ = Use first sampling plan above arrow.

Ac = Acceptance number.

Re = Rejection number.

† = If the acceptance number has been exceeded, but the rejection number has not been reached, accept the lot, but reinstate normal inspection.

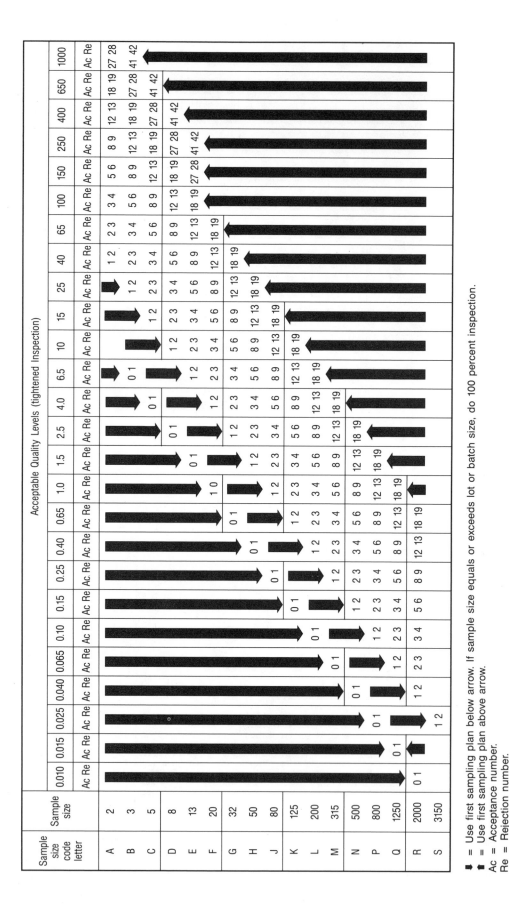

TABLE 10.5   SINGLE SAMPLING PLANS FOR TIGHTENED INSPECTION (MASTER TABLE) (MIL-STD-105D)

➡ = Use first sampling plan below arrow. If sample size equals or exceeds lot or batch size, do 100 percent inspection.

◀ = Use first sampling plan above arrow.

Ac = Acceptance number.

Re = Rejection number.

CHART G — OPERATING CHARACTERISTIC CURVES FOR SINGLE SAMPLING PLANS
(Curves for double and multiple sampling are matched as closely as practicable)

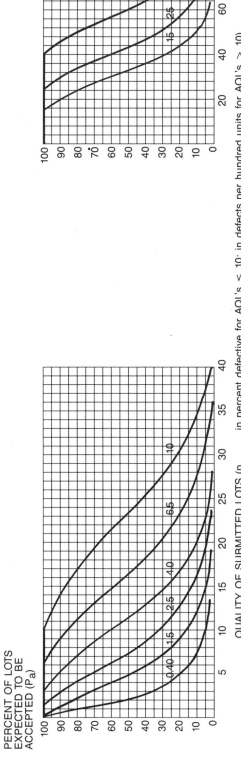

PERCENT OF LOTS EXPECTED TO BE ACCEPTED (P_a)

QUALITY OF SUBMITTED LOTS (p, in percent defective for AQL's ≤ 10; in defects per hundred units for AQL's > 10)

Note: Figures on curves are Acceptable Quality Levels (AQL's) for normal inspection.

TABLE X-G-1 — TABULATED VALUES FOR OPERATING CHARACTERISTIC CURVES FOR SINGLE SAMPLING PLANS

Acceptable Quality Levels (normal inspection)

p (in percent defective)

P_a	0.40	1.5	2.5	4.0	6.5	10
99.0	0.032	0.475	1.38	2.63	5.94	9.75
95.0	0.161	1.13	2.59	4.39	8.50	13.1
90.0	0.329	1.67	3.50	5.56	10.2	15.1
75.0	0.895	3.01	5.42	7.98	13.4	19.0
50.0	2.14	5.19	8.27	11.4	17.5	23.7
25.0	4.23	8.19	11.9	15.4	22.3	29.0
10.0	6.94	11.6	15.8	19.7	27.1	34.1
5.0	8.94	14.0	18.4	22.5	30.1	37.2
1.0	13.5	19.0	23.7	28.0	35.9	43.3
	0.65	2.5	4.0	6.5	10	X

p (in defects per hundred units)

P_a	0.40	1.5	2.5	4.0	6.5	10	15	25	40
99.0	0.032	0.466	1.36	2.57	5.57	9.08	14.9	23.4	39.3
95.0	0.160	1.10	2.55	4.26	8.16	12.4	19.3	28.9	46.5
90.0	0.328	1.66	3.44	5.45	9.85	14.6	21.9	32.2	50.8
75.0	0.900	3.00	5.39	7.92	13.2	18.6	26.9	38.2	58.4
50.0	2.16	5.24	8.35	11.5	17.7	24.0	33.3	45.8	67.7
25.0	4.33	8.41	12.3	16.0	23.2	30.3	40.7	54.4	78.0
10.0	7.19	12.2	16.6	20.9	29.0	36.8	48.1	62.9	88.1
5.0	9.36	14.8	19.7	24.2	32.9	41.1	55.6	68.4	94.5
1.0	14.4	20.7	26.3	31.4	41.0	50.0	63.0	79.5	107
	0.65	2.5	4.0	6.5	10	X	15	25	X

Acceptable Quality Levels (tightened inspection)

Note: Binomial distribution used for percent defective computations; Poisson for defects per hundred units.

TABLE 10.6 TABLES FOR SAMPLE SIZE CODE LETTER: G — MIL-STD-105D

Exercise

Select single sampling plans for normal, reduced, and tightened inspection from MIL-STD-105D for the following data:

Lot size = 200, AQL = 1.5 percent

(Answer: Normal (32, 1, 2); reduced (13, 0, 2); tightened (32, 1, 2)).

SOME NOTES ABOUT SAMPLING PLANS

1. A question that usually arises when using MIL-STD-105D is, what is a good AQL?

   Most companies settle for an AQL value that has proven to be economical over the years. Smaller AQL values will result in large sample sizes and hence increased cost of inspection. Larger values for the AQL might result in lenient plans that might allow more defectives pass through inspection.

   The best AQL value is the tradeoff between the cost of inspection and the cost of not inspecting enough. Mathematical calculations can be made to determine this best value, but it may be easier to start with some value such as 1.0 percent and adjust it based on experience.

   Different AQL values can be used for different products or different characteristics of the same product, depending on the criticality of the characteristic. More critical characteristics/product should be inspected with smaller AQL values.

2. There is a common misconception about sampling plans.

   Suppose we use a sampling plan based on an AQL of 1.5 percent at an incoming inspection station. This does not mean we are accepting batches of parts that are 1.5 percent defective. It only means that lots with 1.5 percent or less defectives will be readily accepted and lots with more than 1.5 percent defects will not be accepted as readily. The average quality of the lots accepted by a plan with AQL 1.5 percent can be expected to be better than 1.5 percent (percent defectives smaller than 1.5 percent) especially if switching rules are applied. These rules put a psychological pressure on the vendor to supply good quality.

3. Sampling plans versus control charts.

   As mentioned in Chapter One, control charts are preventive tools and sampling plans are acceptance tools. However, if the results of sampling inspection are used to find out what went wrong and for taking corrective action, they will also serve the purpose served by control charts.

   Some people believe — in as much as sampling plans are used after the product is produced and certain percent of defectives is accepted—they have no place in the modern quality control systems, which should aim at continuous reduction of product variability and shoot for zero or near zero defective rates. While no one can argue against such goals and the use of control charts to achieve those ends, it must be recognized that a majority of today's industry is far from the ideal condition where they can prove the quality of their products with evidence of control charts. Until such time when all the vendors can do that, many customers will have to depend on sampling plans to verify quality at receiving inspection. It is then necessary to understand how the sampling plans work and how to use them correctly.

4. ANSI/ASQC Standard Z1.4

A standard has been published by the American National Standards Institute in cooperation with the American Society for Quality Control. ANSI/ASQC Z1.4 can be considered a replacement of MIL-STD-105D, with certain improved features.

REVIEW

Sampling plans for attributes and measurements are available with single, double, and multiple samples.

Single sampling plans for attributes are the plans used most often.

OC curves tell us how strict or lenient sampling plans are.

We first specify a desired OC curve by specifying AQL, α or LTPD, β, or both.

The MIL-STD-105D provides sampling plans to satisfy desired AQL requirements.

A single sampling plan can be chosen from MIL-STD-105D if the lot size and desired AQL are known.

BIBLIOGRAPHY

Deming, W. Edwards. *Quality, Productivity, and Competitive Position.* Cambridge: Massachusetts Institute of Technology, 1982.

Duncan, Acheson J. *Quality Control and Industrial Statistics,* 4th ed. Homewood, Ill.: Richard Irwin, Inc., 1974.

Grant, Eugene L., and Richard S. Leavenworth. *Statistical Quality Control,* 5th ed. New York: McGraw-Hill Book Co., 1980.

Hines, Wiliam W., and Douglas C. Montgomery. *Probability and Statistics in Engineering and Management Science,* 2nd ed. New York: John Wiley and Sons, 1972.

Juran, J.M., and Frank M. Gryna, Jr. *Quality Planning and Analysis,* 2nd ed. New York: McGraw-Hill Book Co., 1980.

APPENDIX 1
VARIABLES CONTROL CHART ($\bar{X}$ AND R)

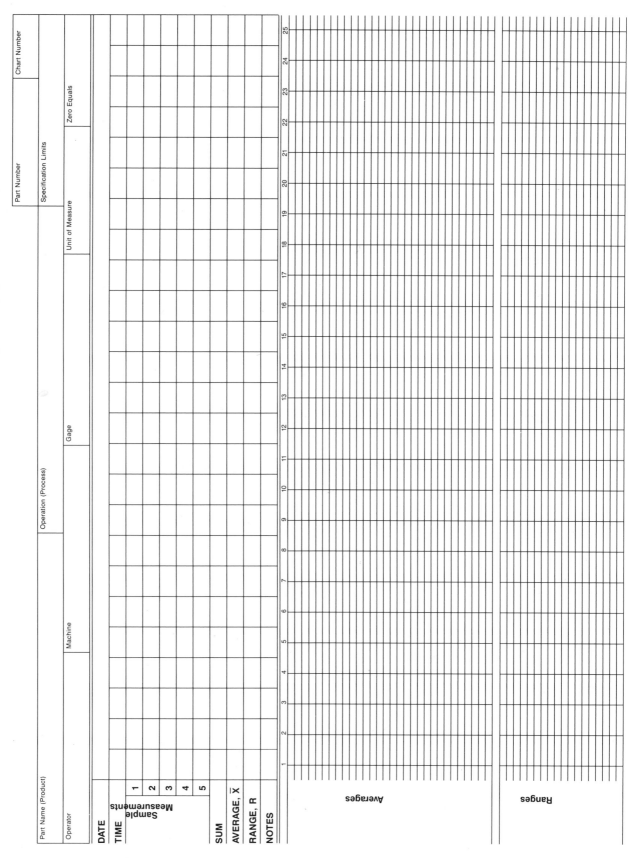

Calculation of Control Limits for X-bar and R-Charts

Product: **Machine:**   **Calculated by:**

$\overline{\overline{X}} = \Sigma \overline{X} / k = $ _____ / _____ = ____
                                    (Sum of all $\overline{X}$'s)   (Number of $\overline{X}$'s added)

$\overline{R} = \Sigma R / k = $ _____ / _____ = ___
                                    (Sum of all Rs)   (Number of Rs added)

Subgroup size: n = ____   Target (if given) = ____

In the formulas for limits use values of D_3, D_4, and A_2 from the table below based on subgroup size. Use $\overline{\overline{X}}$ = Target if one is available. Otherwise use the value computed above.

Limits for R-Chart

$UCL(R) = D_4\overline{R} = $ ____ × ____ = ____
                              (D_4) $(\overline{R})$

$CL(R) = \overline{R} = $ ____

$LCL(R) = D_3\overline{R} = $ ____ × ____ = ____
                              (D_3) $(\overline{R})$

Limits for X̄-Chart

$UCL(\overline{X}) = \overline{\overline{X}} + A_2\overline{R} = $ ____ + ____ × ____ = ____
                              $(\overline{X})$ (A_2) $(\overline{R})$

$CL(\overline{X}) = \overline{\overline{X}} = $ ____

$LCL(\overline{X}) = \overline{\overline{X}} - A_2\overline{R} = $ ____ − ____ × ____ = ____
                              $(\overline{X})$ (A_2) $(\overline{R})$

Factors for Control Chart Limit

Subgroup Size (n)	D_3	D_4	A_2	d_2
2	0	3.268	1.880	1.128
3	0	2.574	1.023	1.693
4	0	2.282	0.729	2.059
5	0	2.114	0.577	2.326
6	0	2.004	0.483	2.534
7	0.076	1.924	0.419	2.704
8	0.136	1.864	0.373	2.847
9	0.184	1.816	0.337	2.970
10	0.223	1.777	0.308	3.078

APPENDIX 2
p-CHART

Product Number: **Machine Number:**   **Date:**   **Inspector:**

Defect Category: **Gage Used:**   **Subgroup Size:**

Subgroup Number	1	2	3	4	5	6	7	8	9	10	11	12	13	14	15	16	17	18	19	20	21	22	23	24	25
Number of Defectives																									
Fraction Defectives, p																									

$$\bar{p} = \Sigma\, p/k = \quad / \quad =$$

$$UCL_p = \bar{p} + 3\sqrt{\bar{p}(1-\bar{p})\,/\,n} =$$

$$LCL_p = \bar{p} - 3\sqrt{\bar{p}(1-\bar{p})\,/\,n} =$$

APPENDIX 3
c-CHART

| Part Number: | | Machine Number: | | Date: | | Inspector: |

| Defect Type: | | Instruments: | | | Unit: | |

Unit Number	1	2	3	4	5	6	7	8	9	10	11	12	13	14	15	16	17	18	19	20	21	22	23	24	25
Number of Defects																									

$$\bar{c} = \Sigma\, c/k = / =$$

$$UCL_c = \bar{c} + 3\sqrt{\bar{c}} =$$

$$LCL_c = \bar{c} - 3\sqrt{\bar{c}} =$$

APPENDIX 4
FREQUENCY DISTRIBUTION DATA SHEET

Part Number	Part Name	Source		
Characteristic		Engineering Specification		
Date	Remarks			

Call Size From - To	Midpoint	Tally	Frequency	Percent Frequency	Cumulative Percent Frequency
		Total		100	

INDEX